T5-AFC-867

Become
A
Home Inspector !

by

Michael A. Pompeii, P.E.

2001 Edition

*A concise guide to starting up and operating
a successful Home Inspection business*

Copyright © 1998, 2001 by Michael A. Pompeii, P.E.
Fredericksburg, VA   22405

2001 Edition

All rights reserved.   No part of this book may be reproduced in any
form or by any means without permission in writing from the author.

The author and publisher do not assume and hereby disclaim any liability
to any party for any loss or damage caused by errors or omissions in
Become A Home Inspector, whether such errors or omissions result from
negligence, accident or any other cause.

ISBN 0-9711954-0-4

Printed in the United States of America

This book is dedicated to Josh, Kasey, and Andrew

Ordering Information:

Additional copies of this book may be ordered from Pompeii Engineers, Attn: Publications, 8 Wolcott Road, Fredericksburg, VA 22405. In your request, include the number of books you wish to purchase and the intended use of the books.

Table of Contents

Chapter 1: INTRODUCTION

This book shows you how to startup and operate a successful home inspection business. The information presented is intended for beginners that desire to startup and operate a home inspection business, as well as seasoned inspectors who wish to increase their knowledge base and to sharpen their business skills.

The somewhat complicated procedures for starting and operating a home inspection business have been broken down into individual steps for you to easily follow in this book. This serves to simplify the overall process in going from a business idea to a viable business. Hopefully, the information in this book will save you thousands of dollars in unnecessary costs, months of research, and answer many questions that you may have about any aspect of the home inspection business.

The information presented in this book is modeled after the success of the author's own home inspection business. This business has operated successfully since 1992 under the format and guidelines presented in this book. Many lessons learned about the home inspection business during this time are incorporated throughout.

This book covers how to set up and operate your business; it does not cover very much technical information on house construction or house maintenance. As such, in addition to this book, it is highly recommended that the reader also obtain, study, and completely understand any materials that deal with the basics of home construction and mechanical, electrical, and plumbing systems. This technical background, along with the information in this book, will form a solid foundation for you to use to open and maintain a successful and highly profitable home inspection business.

1.1 INDUSTRY OVERVIEW

As most people are well aware, home inspections are one of the most rapidly expanding areas of the real estate industry. While almost nonexistent in the 1980's, it is estimated that about 60% of all home sales now include a home inspection. This figure is still growing and is projected to grow even further over the next few years and through the next decade.

The purchase of a home is one of the largest investments that a consumer can make. As such, consumers are turning to home inspectors to provide them "peace of mind" by inspecting their prospective property and alerting them to any problems. The last thing that any home buyer wants is to get stuck with a "lemon".

Most states do not regulate home inspectors. Thus, anyone can hang a sign on their door and call themselves a "Home Inspector". In fact, most home inspectors are former builders or construction workers. Many have never received any formal training in inspection procedures, while others have taken correspondence courses, franchiser courses, or short seminars. All of these training opportunities strive to produce knowledgeable inspectors. However, the quality and longevity of a home inspection business is only as good as the quality and knowledge of its inspectors. This is why you should strive to constantly upgrade your knowledge of home inspection technology by reading pertinent books and magazines and attending seminars and courses to improve your skills.

For persons starting out in the home inspection business, almost everyone has questions about and is concerned with the possibilities of litigation. We live in an extremely litigious environment, and people sue people for any and all reasons, whether they are right or not. This book emphasizes the avoidance of legal problems by helping you inspect the right way and report the right way. YOU MUST ALWAYS BE EXTREMELY CAUTIOUS IN WHAT YOU SAY AND WHAT YOU WRITE TO MINIMIZE THE CHANCE OF LITIGATION. This is extremely important, and will be emphasized throughout this book.

1.2 DESCRIPTION OF SERVICES

As a home inspector, you will provide home inspections to prospective home buyers, home sellers, home owners, realtors, mortgage companies, and the general public. You may also provide consultation services for home buyers, sellers, and owners regarding specific house problems, such as leaky roofs or basements. Other possible services, such as screening for radon, lead, and asbestos require specialized training and licensing, and are beyond the scope of this book.

The complete home inspection procedure presented here is a unique system that methodically covers the house's lot & landscaping, exterior, roofing, foundation, framing, insulation, plumbing, electrical, heating/cooling, kitchen, bathrooms, and safety. A typical complete home inspection for an average home takes about 3 hours to complete. All inspections are visual inspections of readily accessible areas only. No destructive inspections or testing is performed unless specifically authorized in writing by the property owner.

You will report both verbally and in writing to the customer, explaining the good and bad points of the home. A written report, preferably using the copyrighted Pompeii Home Inspection Report, is delivered to the customer immediately after the inspection. Your verbal report to the customer occurs immediately after completion of the written report. <u>You will never make the decision for the customer to buy or not to buy the home</u>; you will only provide information about the home for the customer to make an informed decision for his or her self.

The Pompeii Home Inspection Report is used throughout this book. Seven years of research and lessons-learned have gone into the content and style of this report. It provides a relatively simple, logical, and methodical approach to use when inspecting a home. It also helps you, the inspector, to not miss anything during the inspection. It prompts you with a checklist type format to help ensure each item has been covered in that part of the inspection.

This copyrighted report is available for use in your business. Interested persons can purchase a blank set of forms that comes with a non-transferable Copyright License that allows the inspector to make unlimited copies for his or her company's use. Specific ordering information can be found in Appendix B of this book. A Home Inspection Agreement is included with each report. The Pompeii Home Inspection Report is highly recommended to help minimize your legal risk and to help you perform a high quality, thorough inspection using the home inspection "system" presented in this book.

Chapter 2: BUSINESS STANDARDS

2.1 BUSINESS PHILOSOPHY

Your business philosophy should be to provide the highest quality home inspections possible. Each and every home inspection must be thorough, complete, and to the satisfaction of every customer.

You must uphold the highest levels of professionalism, honesty, and integrity in all areas of the business. This includes conducting inspections, office management, customer relationships, realtor relationships, and dealing with the general public.

If you adhere to this philosophy, there is a high probability that your business will be highly profitable in the long term. But if you fail to follow this philosophy, your chances of mid-term or long-term success in this business are slim to none. All it takes is just a few instances of non-professionalism or dishonesty to give you or your business a poor reputation. Likewise, your continuous professionalism, honesty and integrity will ultimately spread throughout the real estate community in your area, giving you a very good reputation and providing you a very profitable business.

2.2 BUSINESS TYPES

There are several types of business structures that are suitable for a home inspection business. You must choose one of them. They are:

1) Sole Proprietorship

2) Partnership

3) Corporation

4) Limited Liability Company (LLC)

The type of business structure you choose must be based on your own personal situation. There are advantages and disadvantages of each type, and getting into those details are well beyond the scope of this book. For example, a sole proprietorship may be perfect for someone just starting out, working part-time, who does not do a lot of inspections. But under a sole proprietorship, your own personal assets may be at risk. Incorporating your business separates your personal assets from your home inspection business, but the extra paperwork and government oversight of your corporation may not be worth it to you.

You must do thorough research on each type of business, and pick the one that suits your own personal situation the best. There is a lot of information on the internet and in bookstores that deals specifically with helping you to decide what is the best business type for your business. If you are still not comfortable with making the decision yourself, you are encouraged to consult a lawyer who specializes in this area.

2.3 LICENSES AND PERMITS

You must ensure that your business is in compliance with all state and local laws with respect to licenses and permits for operating your business. The two major items here are:

1) Local requirements for operating a business in your city or county.

2) State requirements if your state has or is about to enact licensing of any type for home inspectors.

Almost every city or county requires you to register a business of any type, and a few even have there own requirements for home inspectors. Just contact your county or city government to find out what you need to do. Usually it is just a matter of filling out a simple registration form and paying a minimal registration fee.

Some states regulate (or have certain laws for) home inspectors, while many states have no requirements at all for home inspectors. But every year there are more and more states that are proposing or enacting training, experience, and/or licensing requirements for you to become a home inspector in that state.

As of the writing of this book, here is a list of states that currently have various laws and/or requirements that regulate home inspectors:

ALABAMA	MARYLAND	PENNSYLVANIA
ARIZONA	MASSACHUSETTS	RHODE ISLAND
ARKANSAS	MONTANA	SOUTH CAROLINA
CALIFORNIA	NEW JERSEY	SOUTH DAKOTA

CONNECTICUT	NEVADA	TEXAS
GEORGIA	NORTH CAROLINA	TENNESSEE
LOUISIANA	OREGON	WISCONSIN
KENTUCKY (Lexington only)		

If your state is on this list, you must contact your state government to receive details on their home inspector requirements. If your state is not on this list, then your state does not have any specific training or experience requirements for you to perform home inspections in that state. But please be aware that new states are constantly being added to this list, and new state laws and regulations regarding home inspectors are always being proposed or changed. Therefore, DO NOT RELY ON THIS LIST ALONE. Your state laws may have changed since the writing of this book, so it would be wise to contact your state government anyway, just to be sure.

If your state is on the list, who do you contact in the state government? Here is a current list of phone numbers or web site addresses to try:

ALABAMA	(334) 242-7205
ARIZONA	(602) 542-1525
ARKANSAS	(501) 682-1010
CALIFORNIA	www.state.ca.us
CONNECTICUT	(860) 713-6059
GEORGIA	www.state.ga.us
KENTUCKY	(606) 258-3270 (Lexington only)
LOUISIANA	www.state.la.us
MARYLAND	www.state.md.us

MASSACHUSETTS	(617) 727-7374
MONTANA	www.state.mt.us
NEW JERSEY	(973) 504-6534
NEVADA	(775) 687-4280
NORTH CAROLINA	(919) 733-3901
OREGON	(503) 378-4621
PENNSYLVANIA	www.state.pa.us
RHODE ISLAND	(401) 222-1270
SOUTH CAROLINA	www.state.sc.us
SOUTH DAKOTA	(605) 773-3600
TEXAS	www.state.tx.us
TENNESSEE	www.state.tn.us
WISCONSIN	(608) 266-2112

For the web sites listed, just search for "home inspector" and follow the links to get to the proper department of the state government. If the search comes up empty, at least you may be able to find a phone number to get you started.

For all other states, just go to www.state.xx.us on the internet, but instead of typing in the "xx", substitute you state's two letter abbreviation in for the "xx". For example, Virginia would be www.state.va.us and Florida would be www.state.fl.us.

Because state and local requirements vary widely, you are solely responsible for compliance with their specific applicable laws and regulations, and you must keep informed of any changes in these laws and regulations.

2.4 ORGANIZATIONAL AFFILIATIONS

In the 1970's and 1980's, a lack of training and inspection knowledge gave home inspectors, in general, a bad name. To help rectify this situation, various trade groups were organized to set standards for home inspections. Most notable is the American Society of Home Inspectors (ASHI). ASHI has numerous publications available, including their standards of practice. Another organization, the National Association of Home Inspectors (NAHI), also has published guidelines for the home inspection industry. You are encouraged to obtain and completely understand these standards.

If you are a licensed Professional Engineer or licensed Architect, it would be to your advantage to join the National Society of Professional Engineers (NSPE) or the American Institute of Architects (AIA), and other well-known professional engineering or architectural organizations (ASME, ASCE, ASEE, etc.). There is also an organization for inspectors who are licensed engineers called NABIE (National Association of Building Inspection Engineers).

Affiliation with a recognized organization gives you a distinct advantage over your competitors, especially in advertising (in the yellow pages, brochures, flyers, etc,). Customers want to see affiliations with national organizations because it makes them more secure in their selection of a home inspector.

You should also join your local Board of Realtors Association (or similar organization). Your company name, address, and phone number will be published in the area's multiple listing service book or computer system, along with other inspectors. Since most real estate agents copy this page and provide it to their home-buying customers, this is a very important organization to join. You will probably receive a lot of business through this listing!

2.5 INSURANCE

There are three types of insurance that you should consider carrying, namely vehicle insurance, errors and omissions, and business liability.

You should carry insurance on your company vehicle. Many states specify minimum levels of liability insurance that must be carried, but you are encouraged to carry as much insurance as you can reasonably afford. This helps protect both your business and your personal financial health. This business vehicle insurance is available through most local insurance agents.

In order to help protect yourself from lawsuits from customers where you made (or were alleged to have made) errors and/or omissions during a home inspection, many home inspectors like to carry "Errors & Omissions" insurance. This is usually referred to as "E&O insurance". Most states do not require home inspectors to carry E&O insurance, but you are encouraged to do so, especially if you perform a large number of inspections. The more inspections you perform, the higher the probability that you may miss something that a customer would hold you liable for. Keep in mind that most customers will choose not to litigate due to the high costs of litigation and the high probability that they may lose.

You will probably not be able to find any local insurance companies that will carry E&O insurance for home inspectors. National organizations like ASHI or NAHI may have

E&O insurance carriers set up to provide this coverage to you at discounted rates. Another popular insurance company for E&O coverage for home inspectors is through the Foundation of Real Estate Appraisers (FREA), located at 4907 Morena Boulevard, Suite 1415, San Diego, CA, 92117. The phone number for information is 1-800-882-4410. A typical E&O policy will cost you approximately $800 to $1200 per year, and you receive $300,000 to $1,000,000 of professional E&O liability insurance with a $1,000 deductible.

You may also consider purchasing business liability insurance in case you or someone you are with is injured during the course of a home inspection. This type of insurance can be carried through a local insurance agent. Keep in mind that claims for injuries received on a property are usually covered by the homeowner's or property owner's insurance coverage; however, there are times when no homeowner's insurance policies are in effect when you perform the inspection.

2.6 ADVERTISING AND MARKETING

THE EFFECTIVE ADVERTISING AND MARKETING OF YOUR SERVICES IS CRUCIAL TO THE SUCCESS OF YOUR BUSINESS. You can be the best home inspector in your state, but if nobody knows about you, nobody will hire you.

Marketing and advertising is especially necessary during your business start-up. Once you become firmly established, your reputation as a good inspector will become your major marketing tool. However, you will ALWAYS need to have a balanced marketing plan to keep up with the competition.

There are a number of ways to effectively market your business. The best marketing plan for a home inspection business is very broad and covers many angles. The major items in this marketing plan follow:

1) Keep your name in front of real estate agents. Visit all real estate offices in your territory at least once every two months to place brochures, flyers, or business cards in each agent's mailbox and in any brochure display in each office. Make sure your brochures and flyers are well stocked and in a prominent position among the competition's brochures. Talk to brokers and offer to give informational presentations at weekly sales meetings where all the real estate agents are present; try to do this once a year at each real estate office. If you can gain referrals on a consistent basis from just a few high-volume real estate agents, you will most likely get all the inspections you can handle.

2) Join the local board of realtors association as an affiliate member. This will get your business listed in the local Multiple Listing Service (MLS) book and/or computer system that all real estate offices carry. All real estate listings in the area are listed in this book, and it receives heavy usage from real estate agents. This book is usually updated every two weeks. Many times, when a realtor's client asks that a home inspection be performed before the sale, the realtor will copy the page of "Home Inspectors" from the MLS book and let the client choose their own inspector. Make sure your company's name is in there!

3) Advertise in the Yellow Pages of the phone directory in your area. Research is conclusive that the bigger and more prominent the Yellow Pages ad, the more business you will receive. You choose the size of your Yellow Pages ad, but a "quarter column" ad may be large enough. Be careful what ad size you choose, because the cost of the ad gets

a lot higher as the ad size increases. The cost of these advertisements vary according to the size of the directory area. Surprisingly, you will probably not receive as much business as you think you may through this method! Personal experience has shown that this is not the most cost effective form of advertising for this type of business. But if you live in a small town and have the only ad, you may do well with this type of advertising.

4) Pass out your business cards to your customers and real estate agents at the inspection, and give cards to friends and acquaintances as you deem appropriate. When you perform a good home inspection, customers and realtors will keep your business card handy and will refer you to their home-buying friends and relatives. The longer you are in business, the more effective this "network" of customers becomes in providing you business.

5) Advertise in the real estate section of local newspapers. Use display ads to get your name in front of prospective home buyers who are scanning the houses for sale that are listed here. Most newspapers carry their "major" real estate section one day a week (usually Friday, Saturday, or Sunday). The relatively inexpensive cost of a small display ad for one day a week in this section is very cost-effective in generating business. Advertising in the classified section of newspapers is discouraged due to its limited effectiveness.

6) Place flyers that advertise "1-Year Warranty Inspections" in the mailboxes or newspaper boxes of new houses in recently developed subdivisions or housing areas. Builders almost always provide 1-year warranties to new home buyers, and many of these buyers will turn to home inspectors to make a list of problems with the house that the builder would repair for free while the house is still under warranty. This is a very cost effective method to increase your business.

2.7 ACCOUNTING AND RECORDKEEPING

ACCOUNTING

You must record and keep records of all income and expenses. An easy, inexpensive way to do this is by using simple off-the-shelf software, such as Quicken or Microsoft Money. This software is a powerful, easy to use, time saving method for recording and reporting all financial transactions, and is suited perfectly for this type of business. The automatic reporting ability of this type of software is especially useful for preparing financial reports and tax returns.

In your accounting system, the recommended categories for expenses should be as follows: Advertising, Vehicle Expenses, Utilities, Office Supplies, Office Equipment, Inspection Equipment, Insurance, Professional Dues, Trade Journals, Continuing Education, and Miscellaneous. You may also add other categories as you deem appropriate. There must be only one category for income. The arrangement of income and expenses in this way will greatly simplify completion of your tax returns.

Remember, YOU are solely responsible for the completeness and accuracy of recording all financial transactions.

RECORDKEEPING

You must keep and appropriately file all written receipts of income, expenses, and any other financial transaction. These are required for tax purposes and possible IRS audits. All income and expense records must also be recorded as outlined in the Accounting section, above.

Records for each and every home inspection must also be kept. After each inspection is completed, you can assemble the record of the inspection as follows:

1) Keep the duplicate Inspection Report cover page. It contains all the important information of the inspection and of the customer.

2) At the top right corner of this cover page, write in the money amount received for the inspection and the number of miles traveled for the inspection.

3) Assemble the inspection record with the cover page on top; next, your white copy of the inspection agreement; next, the copy of the phone record for the customer, and finally any other documentation received from anyone involved in the inspection (realtor's business cards, multiple listing service sheet, etc.). If desired, you may also attach a copy of the inspection sheets.

4) File this record appropriately with other home inspection records for that month or year. A sample inspection record is shown on the next page for reference. KEEP THESE RECORDS PERMANENTLY.

Remember, YOU are solely responsible for the completeness and appropriate filing of all business and inspection records.

ABC HOME INSPECTION SERVICE, INC.

MONTHLY RECORD

1. Date: _____

2. Reporting Period (month/year): _____ , 20___

3. Listing of Inspections/Consultations and Gross Income:

Inspection #	Customer Last Name	Gross Income ($)

(Continue as necessary)

17

2.8 BANKING PROCEDURES

You must open up a business checking or savings account at a local, convenient bank. Banks have different requirements and procedures for opening accounts; check with your specific bank.

In a business checking account, there are many types of business checks available. In the interest of simplicity, it is recommend you choose a simple, personal-type of checkbook that you can easily carry around with you. Larger, fancier, ledger type checkbooks are too large and bulky for this type of business.

All inspection fees and any other fee that you collect should be deposited in full in your account. If you need cash, then just deposit the fees and then make an immediate withdrawal. The purpose for depositing checks (and not just cashing them) is to keep a running log of your income. This makes it easy to compare your income records with the automatic records you receive monthly from your bank.

You must keep and file all of your bank statements. They serve as solid evidence in the event of an IRS audit.

CHAPTER 3:   OPERATING STANDARDS

3.1 OFFICE EQUIPMENT

The following office equipment and office supplies are recommended for your home inspection business. Requirements and specifications of each item are included with each listed item.

1. <u>TELEPHONE</u>

Requirements: - Must be high quality

                       - No speakerphones

                       - Must have "hold" button feature

2. <u>TELEPHONE ANSWERING MACHINE</u>

Requirements: - Must be high quality

                       - Must have digital outgoing/incoming messages (no

                         cassettes; too unreliable)

                       - Must have time/date stamp feature

                       - Must have remote access

3. <u>COMPUTER</u> (optional)

Requirements: - latest processor

                       - Adequate hard drive space for software

4. <u>COMPUTER SOFTWARE</u> (optional)

Requirements: - Word processor (WordPerfect, MS Word, MS

                     Works, or similar)

                - Bookkeeping and reporting software (Microsoft

                     Money, Quicken, or similar). This will save you a

                     LOT of time and effort at tax time!

5. <u>LASER PRINTER</u> (optional)

Requirements: - Dot matrix printers not recommended due to print

                     quality

                - High quality inkjets acceptable

                - Capable of printing letters, envelopes, and labels

6. <u>FAX MACHINE</u> (optional)

Requirements: - Computer fax preferred (it's free at eFax.com)

                - Low cost thermal machine acceptable

                - Answering machine hookup capability

7. <u>MISCELLANEOUS OFFICE SUPPLIES</u>

      a. Letterhead Paper   - Must be high quality

                                 - Use for all correspondence

      b. Mailing Envelopes   - Regular 4" x 11.5" (approx.)

                                 - Matches letterhead

                                 - Return address may be printed or

                                   stamped

c. Large Envelopes	- 9" x 12" (approx.) manila envelopes
	- Used for mailing reports & documents
d. Laser Paper	- 8.5" x 11" size
	- As needed for printer
e. Fax Paper	- As needed for fax machine
f. 3.5" Diskettes	- As needed for computer
g. Telephone Questionnaires	- Sample copy provided in this book
	- Used when responding to inspection inquiry calls
	- Need one per inquiry call
h. Files	- Use for organization of business records and functions
	- As needed for your office system
i. General Office Supplies	- Pens, scissors, stapler, tape, etc.
	- As needed for your office system

3.2 INSPECTION EQUIPMENT

The following inspection equipment, inspection tools, and inspection supplies are recommended for your home inspection business. Critical specifications and characteristics of each item are included with each item.

ITEM	SPECIFICATIONS
1. 16 foot Extension Ladder	- Aluminum Type III (for light weight) - Heavier Type I/II wood or fiberglass acceptable - 8 ft collapsed length, 12 ft working length - May substitute folding-type ladder
2. 6 foot Stepladder	- Aluminum Type III (for light weight) - Heavier Type I/II wood or fiberglass acceptable (but relatively heavy and hard to maneuver in houses)
3. Toolbox	- Plastic preferred (for light weight) - Dimensions approx. 20"L x 10"W x 10"H or similar
4. Tool Pouch & Belt	- 1 large pocket (approx. 5" x 7") - 1 small pocket (approx. 4" x 4")

- Slots for 2 screwdrivers

- Slots for 1 pliers

- Large comfortable belt

5. Knee Pads

- Used for inspecting crawlspaces

- Hard plastic caps over nylon-type
  supports

- 2 Velcro closures per knee

- Get the best ones you can buy; you'll be
  glad you did!

6. Coveralls

- Used for inspecting crawlspaces

- Larger size to easily fit over clothes

- Zipper in front

- Durable, lightweight material

- Must be easy to put on and take off

- Long sleeves

- Machine washable, wrinkle free type

7. Hat

- Used for inspecting crawlspaces

- Keeps cobwebs off of hair/head

- Baseball-type cap acceptable

8. Dust Masks

- Used for inspecting attics and
  crawlspaces

- Surgical type masks acceptable

23

- Not for use in chemical vapor
  environments!
- Carried in toolbox

9. Boots
- Construction worker type boots
- High or low rise
- Must be waterproof and easily cleaned

10. Shirts
- Polo type cotton knit shirts for warm
  weather use
- Recommended quantity: at least 2 per
  inspector

11. Jacket
- Cotton lined windbreaker-type for
  cool/cold weather
- Recommended quantity: 1 per
  inspector

12. Rain Suit
- Disposable plastic type with hood is
  recommended
- Carry at least 2; one for you, one to
  lend to client (if needed)

13. Gloves
- Lightweight cotton or leather
- Recommended quantity: 2 per
  inspector

- Carried in toolbox

- Used when you go in crawlspaces

14. Elastic Cords

- Elastic, bungee-type

- Used to hold down ladders

- Quantity/Size: As applicable

15. Briefcase

- Standard size, approx. 18"L x 13"H x
    3.5"D

- At least 2 large document pockets

16. Clipboards

- Standard letter size

- Must be high quality

- Get a separate one with a rain
    shield/cover to use when it rains

- Carried in briefcase

17. Binoculars

- Used for inspecting roof areas

- 10X power (or more) required

- Carrying case required

- Carried in toolbox

18. Flashlight

- Must be high quality!

- 2 "D" battery size

- Halogen type bulb recommended

- Carried in large pocket of tool pouch

19. Lantern Flashlight

- Must be high quality!
- One 9-volt lantern battery size
- Used in attics, basements, crawlspaces
- Halogen type bulb recommended
- Carried in toolbox

20. Stud Sensor

- Hand-held electronic type
- Used for locating hidden wall studs
- Must be high quality
- Carried in large pocket of tool pouch

21. Circuit Tester

- 3 prong, 3 light (orange-orange-red)
- Small, hand-held
- Must have GFCI test button
- Carried in small pocket of tool pouch

22. Compass

- Small, handheld Scout-type compass
- Must be high quality
- Used for accurate direction finding at
  homesite
- Carried in small pocket of tool pouch

23. Torpedo Level

- Dimensions approx. 6"L x 1"H
- Used for determining level/plumb of
  walls, slabs, slopes, etc.
- Carried in large pocket of tool pouch

24. Flat Screwdriver

- Standard-type, approx. 7" total length

- Flat blade

- Carried in right-side slot #1 of tool pouch

25. Phillips Screwdriver

- Standard-type, approx. 7" total length

- Phillips blade

- Carried in right-side slot #2 of tool pouch

26. Needle-nose Pliers

- Standard needle-nose type, approx. 7" total length

- Carried in left side slot of tool pouch

27. Adjustable Wrenches

- One approx. 8 inch, one approx. 12 inch

- Carried in toolbox

28. Tape Measure

- Lightweight, 16 foot retractable, stiff-blade tape

- Used for measuring joist, joist spans, and insulation depth

- Carried in large pocket of tool pouch

29. Hand Shovel

- Standard garden-type handheld shovel

- Approx. 12" total length

- Carried in toolbox

27

- Used for clearing surface dirt around
  foundation, if necessary

30. Voltmeter

- Handheld, dimensions approx. 5"L x
  3"W x 1"D
- 2 wire test leads
- Used for determining live/dead circuit
  wires
- Carried in toolbox

31. Moisture Meter

- Handheld, dimensions approx. 5"L x
  3"W x 1"D
- 2-prong probe with coiled lead wire
- Used for determining age of leaks and
  degree of rot in framing members
- Available from Professional
  Equipment, Inc., phone 1-800-334-
  9291, approx. $60.00
- Carried in toolbox

32. Temperature Probe

- Must have fast response time
  (electronic)
- Temperature range at least 32°F to
  120°F
- Used for testing heating/cooling
  system output

- Carried in toolbox

33. Radon Test Canisters

- 48 hour test canisters
- Requires 2 canisters per screening (only if you offer radon testing)
- Some states require licensing for radon!

34. Report Covers

- Recommend easy snap center binder
- Holds up to 30 pages
- Clear front cover, black or dark blue back cover
- Available in office supply stores
- Need 1 per inspection
- Carried in briefcase

35. Business Cards

- Must be high quality!
- Handed out before inspections to all parties (clients, realtors, etc.)
- Carried in briefcase

36. State License (if necessary)

- State home inspector, P.E. or Architect license with plastic cover
- Shown to clients prior to inspection
- Carried in briefcase

37. Pens

- Black ink only, non-erasable

- Must be high quality
- Need one pen plus 2 spares
- Carried in briefcase

38. Inspection Agreement

- One page home inspection agreement
- Must be printed on two-part carbonless paper, top white page for you, yellow bottom page to customer
- Both you and customer must sign
- Available with the Pompeii Home Inspection Report Copyright License
- Copies carried in briefcase
- Need 1 per inspection

39. Pompeii Inspection Report (or similar)

- 16-18 pages per report
- You fill in during inspection process
- Copies carried in briefcase
- Need 1 per inspection

40. Professional Seal (if P.E. or Architect)

- P.E. or Architect stamp for finished inspection report
- IMPORTANT: If you are a licensed engineer or architect, you MUST stamp each home inspection report, or you will be in big trouble with your state!!
- Must meet state requirements

- Includes name and state license
  number
- Carried in briefcase

41. Stamp Ink Pad

- Used for stamping seal on finished
  reports (only if P.E. or Architect)
- Must be black ink
- Carried in briefcase

42. Engineering Paper Pad

- Standard engineering or grid paper
- 8.5" x 11" size
- Used for notes and explanations
- Carried in briefcase

43. Vehicle Signs

- Can be permanent (painted) or
  magnetic (removable)
- At least 10" x 20" in size
- At least one sign per vehicle door
- Sign should display company name, logo
  and local phone number
- Need at least two signs per vehicle

44. Territory Maps

- Must have detailed street/road maps
  your of entire territory
- Available at local book stores

45. Receipt Book	- General purpose receipt book
	- Available in office supply stores
	- Carried in briefcase
	- Give receipt only when requested

46. Large Envelopes	- Approx. 9" x 12" size
	- Used for delivering reports
	- Keep two in briefcase

47. Invoices	- Available in office supply stores
	- Used for billing customers
	- Carried in briefcase

3.3 COMPANY VEHICLE

A company vehicle is required to transport the inspector and his equipment to the inspection site. This vehicle should be a van, pickup truck, or utility vehicle that is capable of carrying the required inspection equipment and to present a professional appearance. In order to keep the initial business start-up costs low, it is recommended that a currently owned vehicle be used.

However, there are some general requirements for any company vehicle. The vehicle must be:

1) a clean late model vehicle in excellent condition

2) no dents, scratches, or accident damage

3) excellent exterior paint condition

4) excellent mechanical condition

5) No bumper stickers or window stickers (besides
   registration)

6) No extraneous novelty items (fuzzy dice, fancy attire, etc.)

7) No interior tears or major wear

8) Any other item that does not present a professional
   appearance to the general public.

In addition, the vehicle must be kept clean and neat, inside and out, to maintain a professional and business-like appearance to customers and the general public. Remember, when you use your company vehicle, you are representing the image of your company to the general public.

When driving the company vehicle, you must show extra courtesy and respect for other drivers. For example, be extra careful not to speed, run red or yellow lights, tailgate, or complete any action that even gives the appearance of an irresponsible driver. Most of all, don't ever get into a traffic argument, confrontation, or exchange gestures with anyone while you or your employees are operating the company vehicle. Again, remember that the other angry driver only sees the signs on your vehicle, and no good will come from it. It can only cause damage to your business.

3.4 BUSINESS HOURS

You must set business hours that are reasonable and convenient to your customers.

If no one is present in your office, your answering machine must be turned on and ready to receive messages 24 hours a day. You should check for messages regularly, and should return any and all phone calls promptly (within at least 24 hours).

You can schedule home inspection appointments at the convenience of your and your customer's schedules. However, you must allow sufficient time between inspections to account for travel time, traffic conditions, and the possibility of running overtime in your first inspection. In general, it is best to schedule about 3.5 to 4 hours between inspections. For most inspectors, 3 complete home inspections per day is the recommended maximum workload for each inspector.

When scheduling inspections in the afternoon, be sure to consider the amount of daylight left in the day. The last scheduled inspection should start at least 3 hours before sunset.

3.5 SETTING INSPECTION FEES

The fees charged for complete home inspections generally depends on what your local competition is charging. Call your competitors on an anonymous basis, or collect their brochures from real estate offices to get a general idea of the price range. You need to set your fees in the same price range. In most areas, the average fee ranges from $200 to $275 per inspection.

Some inspectors set their fees according to the selling price of the home. This is not a good idea because the selling price does not take into account the size of the home, the age of the home, or the location of the home.

Therefore, your pricing policy should be based on 3 things:

1) the size of the home
2) the age of the home
3) the location of the home

Using this criteria: 1) the larger the home (in square feet of the living area), the higher the fee because a larger home requires more time to inspect; 2) the older the home, the higher the fee because an older home requires more time to inspect; and 3) the farther away the home is, the higher the fee because of the increased time you spend on the road.

To set your pricing policy for your specific area, first set your base price using a "base" house. For example, assume a base house is 2000 square feet, less than 10 years old, and is located close to your office. For this base house, a good base price is $200, but may have to be adjusted higher or lower, according to the competition in your local area.

Next factor in the other variables. These cost factors are not strict requirements and are only guidelines for helping you to set fair and appropriate fees.

A) SIZE: - Add $25 if between 2100 and 2400 square feet.

                - Add $50 if between 2500 and 3000 square feet.

                - Add more if over 3000 square feet.

B) AGE: - Add $25 if between 10 and 20 years old.

                - Add $50 or more if over 20 years old.

C) LOCATION: - Add $25 if about 20 miles away.

                - Add $50 or more depending on distance

These extra fees should not be cumulative, or you may end up pricing yourself out of the home inspection business. The maximum additional charge can be about $75 over the base fee, but again it depends on your local competition. For example, the fee for a 2600 square foot home, 15 years old, and 22 miles away may be calculated as follows:

Base	=	$200
Size	=	+ 50
Age	=	+ 25
Location	=	+ 25

Total	=	$300

This fee of $300 will probably be too high, so you would quote $250 for this inspection. Again, THE FEES YOU QUOTE MUST BE CLOSE TO THE COMPETITOR'S FEES IN YOUR AREA.

There are, of course, exceptions to the maximum fee. For example, a house that is extremely run down or is over 100 years old will require setting higher fees. You must use your own judgement in setting these types of fees.

You will also receive calls for partial inspections covering only one or two items, like cracks in walls, wet basements, leaking roofs, etc. The recommended minimum for these types of inspections is about $100. This basic minimum charge includes driving time, up to 45 minutes on site, and delivery of a two (or more) page on-site report (using the appropriate single section(s) of the full report). Any amount less than $100 may not be considered appropriate compensation for your time and effort. This fee may have to be adjusted upward according to the extent of the problem and the complexity of the report. The recommended charge (over the base fee) for this type of inspection can be about $50 per hour for on-site inspection time _and_ for time spent writing the report.

3.6 TELEPHONE PROCEDURES

Most, if not all, of your business will come via your telephone. Thus, YOUR TELEPHONE IS YOUR BUSINESS LIFELINE. You and your employees must always speak clearly, pleasantly, and professionally when conducting any business dealings over the phone.

To maintain a professional image, a dedicated business phone number is required for your office. You should not use your home phone, unless you are prepared to answer it entirely as a business phone. Also, a business phone is required to advertise in the Yellow Pages. You may also want to have a dedicated fax number, or you can get a fax machine or switchbox that automatically detects incoming voice or fax tones and routes them to the phone, answering machine, fax, or modem.

You are encouraged to get "Call Waiting" with your business phone. This is to prevent missing any possible inquiries for home inspections.

You or your employees should PERSONALLY answer the phone whenever possible. Do not let the answering machine answer all the calls. In the home inspection business, many people call around for information on home inspections and very often go with the first company that does not answer with an answering machine! However, the answering machine is still a critical and extremely useful item for your business; let it do its job when you or your employees are not in the office.

Check your answering machine often for messages. Again, in the home inspection business, many people make appointments with the first company that returns their call. Therefore, IT IS EXTREMELY IMPORTANT TO RETURN INQUIRY CALLS AS SOON AS POSSIBLE.

The content and tone of your answering machine greeting is extremely important. When recording this greeting, always speak in a pleasant and friendly tone of voice. A sample message follows:

"HELLO. YOU HAVE REACHED THE OFFICE OF _____ HOME INSPECTION SERVICE. WE SPECIALIZE IN COMPLETE HOME INSPECTIONS FOR HOME BUYERS, AND ALSO PROVIDE CONSULTING SERVICES TO HOME OWNERS. IF YOU WOULD LIKE TO SCHEDULE A HOME

INSPECTION, OR WOULD LIKE MORE INFORMATION ON HOME INSPECTIONS, PLEASE LEAVE YOUR NAME AND PHONE NUMBER AFTER THE TONE, AND WE WILL RETURN YOUR CALL AS SOON AS POSSIBLE. THANKS!"

Your answering machine should have digital incoming and outgoing messages (for clarity and reliability), and a time/date stamp for each message. This lets you know exactly when they called.

When answering or responding to a home inspection inquiry call, you must use one Phone Record Form for each call. A sample form is shown on the next page. Fill in the form while you are speaking to the customer. Keep all filled out forms for your records. Phone Record Forms that had a home inspection will be filed with the inspection record. Phone Record Forms that did not have an inspection will be filed together for possible future reference.

PHONE RECORD FORM

Date: _____

Time: _____ AM / PM

Name: _____

Phone #: (Day) _____

(Eve.) _____

Caller's Inquiry: _____

_____

_____

Home Information: SIZE = _____ square feet

AGE = _____ years

LOCATION = _____

Price quoted: $ _____

Appointment: Day:_____ Date:_____ Time:_____AM/PM

Additional Home Information: _____

_____

_____

_____

Directions to Home (if needed): _____

_____

_____

_____

3.7 APPEARANCE OF INSPECTORS

You and your employees must maintain a clean, well-groomed appearance at all times when performing inspections, interfacing with the public, and interfacing with other business persons. This presents a quality appearance and image to the public.

When performing inspections, all inspectors must present a clean, neat, and professional appearance. You are encouraged to use customized shirts and jackets with your company name and logo attached. One company that provides this customized clothing is Wearguard; go to www.wearguard.com for more information. This type of clothing serves to enhance and standardize the image, product, and format of your business.

You should also consider wearing clean, full-rise workboots. These boots present a "construction official" type of professional image to clients. Many inspection sites will be muddy due to new construction, so you must also wear appropriate socks because you may have to take off your muddy boots when you go indoors.

3.8 BUSINESS ETIQUETTE

You and all of your employees must maintain high standards of professionalism, integrity, honesty, and demeanor in all aspects of the business. All persons that come in contact with the business in any way (including customers, potential customers, realtors, builders, contractors, construction officials, and any other person or persons) MUST be treated with professional courtesy and respect.

You should not operate any other business, nor be associated with any other business, nor make referrals to any other business that presents a conflict of interest OR EVEN GIVES THE APPEARANCE of a conflict of interest to providing a completely objective inspection of any property for any customer. Examples of businesses that interfere with an objective inspection include real estate agents, painting contractors, plumbing contractors, electricians, and any other trade that could possibly benefit from the inspection.

If the client presses you for a referral, simply state that it is company policy not to give referrals because it could possibly interfere with a completely objective inspection, and tell them that the best thing to do is call at least three contractors, get three estimates, and use their best judgement to choose a contractor. This also relieves you of any financial burden or embarrassment if your referral performed a lousy job for your client!!!

3.9 INTERACTING WITH REAL ESTATE AGENTS (REALTORS)

Whenever a realtor calls you to arrange an inspection, make the experience as easy as possible on the realtor by: 1) arranging an appointment that meets the realtors schedule, 2) showing up early at the inspection, 3) performing a good inspection, and 4) treating the customer and realtor with professional courtesy and respect. This will help ensure repeat referrals from realtors, and spread your good name around the real estate office.

If a realtor or any other person ever asks you to "overlook" any problems or tries to sway your judgement in any way, DON'T DO IT!!! Simply explain to the realtor or person that you work for the client, and only the client, and that you would be exposing yourself to almost certain litigation. Repeat- NEVER LET ANYONE SWAY YOUR

JUDGEMENT ON ANY INSPECTION. If the realtor or person is upset with your response and threatens to quit providing you referrals, then politely tell them that you are a professional and that is their decision. Consider yourself lucky not to get any more referrals from that realtor, because you would probably end up in legal trouble sooner or later with them.

Many times the realtor, the seller, or another interested person may ask you for a copy of an inspection report. DO NOT GIVE THE REPORT TO ANY PERSON EXCEPT THE PERSON THAT HIRED YOU AND PAID YOU. Politely explain that this is company policy, and that they should contact the person who hired you to get a copy of the report.

CHAPTER 4: PRE-INSPECTION PROCEDURES

4.1 PRE-INSPECTION PREPARATIONS

This section describes how to prepare for a typical home inspection. Prior to leaving your office to perform inspections, you must prepare for the inspection as follows:

1) <u>Prepare your briefcase</u>. Your briefcase should contain the following:

    A) One (1) blank copy of the Pompeii Inspection Report (or similar) for each inspection scheduled that day.

    B) A file folder with extra copies of the Pompeii Inspection Report (or similar, in case you make a mistake on the original).

    C) One (1) report cover for each scheduled inspection.

    D) One filled-out Home Inspection Agreement (except for signatures) for each scheduled inspection. (Also carry extra copies, just in case.)

    E) Your clipboard.

    F) Your P.E. or Architect stamp and ink pad (if applicable).

    G) At least two high quality pens (black ink).

    H) Each applicable telephone form that scheduled the inspection(s).

    I) A supply of your business cards.

    J) An 8.5" x 11" engineering paper tablet (for explanations to client).

K) Maps/map books of the areas where the inspections are located
(make sure you review these maps before you leave!).

L) A bound, blank copy of the Pompeii Inspection Report (or similar,
to be used to explain the report and inspection procedures to
your client).

2) Prepare your clipboard. Assemble materials on your clipboard, from the bottom up, as follows: 1) a blank copy of the Pompeii Inspection Report (or similar); 2) the filled out copy (except signatures) of the Home Inspection Agreement; 3) your P.E. or architects license (if applicable); and 4) your business card.

3) Prepare your inspection tools and equipment. Make sure your tool belt and toolbox are properly equipped in accordance with the equipment listed previously in this book. Check your flashlights to see if fresh batteries are needed. Also check any other equipment that requires batteries. It's always a good idea to carry extra batteries in your toolbox. If the weather forecast is rain, make sure you bring your portable rainsuits (one for you, one for your client) and possibly an umbrella.

4) Prepare your company vehicle. Load your toolbelt, toolbox, and any other equipment (as specified previously) into your vehicle. Make sure your vehicle is clean, mud-free, and presents a professional image to the public. Attach magnetic signs (unless permanent markings already exist). Reset the odometer to zero to record mileage for the day.

4.2 PUNCTUALITY

Simply stated, ALWAYS arrive a few minutes early at the inspection site and NEVER be late for an inspection.

When you arrive early, you have a chance to get a "feel" for the property. If the home is occupied, knock on the door and let the homeowner know that you are meeting your client (give client's name) for an inspection, and you will wait outside until the client arrives. While waiting for your client, start looking around and start the inspection of the lot, exterior, and roofing.

Arriving late for an inspection is one of the worst mistakes you can make. The clients are anxious, the realtor is in a hurry, and you immediately give a bad impression and start the inspection off on the wrong foot. The impression you must give is one of an orderly, organized, efficient, and professional person. Being late presents the opposite impression. If you are going to be late for any reason, you must contact the client at the earliest possible time to let them know.

In other words, NEVER BE LATE FOR AN APPOINTMENT. This is extremely important to your business and your reputation!

4.3 INITIAL MEETING WITH CLIENT

This section specifies one standard format that each inspector should use when meeting the client at the inspection site. It is extremely important that you always speak clearly and intelligently. Remember- you never get a second chance to make a good first impression!

1) SMILE. Always greet everyone at the inspection site with a big smile. This is extremely important. It not only "breaks the ice", but it immediately presents a friendly, caring attitude to a nervous and anxious client. The importance of this initial smile cannot be emphasized enough!

2) NO BAD BREATH. Chew a breath mint or use a breath spray just before you meet any client. You will be talking face to face, and bad breath is a real turn-off to clients and does not present a professional image.

3) INTRODUCE YOURSELF. Put out your hand for a handshake, smile, and say: **"Hi. I'm (first and last name)."** Always give a firm, but not tight, handshake. This projects sincerity. Person responds with his/her name. Then you respond: **"Nice to meet you."** If desired, engage in some 'small talk'.

4) EXPLAIN WHAT YOU ARE GOING TO DO. The following words and actions are recommended for you to use immediately following the introductions:

"First, let me give you my card." Hand card(s) to client [and realtor]. If you are a P.E. or Architect, use the following: **"Next, let me show you a copy of my state license."** If applicable, hand your license to the client for their review. **"It says that I'm currently licensed in (your state) as a (Professional Engineer or Architect or Home Inspector** [if applicable]**)."** Let the client examine it for a few moments. Make sure you

48

get it back. Offering to show your license provides a certain degree of reassurance to a nervous client.

Put the clipboard down and pick up the bound, blank report. Then say: **"This is a what you'll be getting when I'm finished in two to three hours."** Show the bound report. **"This is a blank copy of your Home Inspection Report. It has a cover page** (show cover page) **and is divided into different sections for each part of the inspection. The sections are Lot & Landscaping** (show Lot & Landscaping page for a few seconds), **Exterior** (show Exterior page for a few seconds), **Roofing, Foundation, Framing, Insulation, Electrical, Plumbing, Heating/Cooling, Interior, Kitchen, Bathrooms, and finally a Safety check."** Flip through each page and pause for a few seconds at each page. Make sure client sees the pages clearly.

Put the bound report down at your side (while still in your hand) for a moment and say: **"I have a very detailed and methodical way in which I will perform the inspection. I'll start with the outside, making three or four trips around the house, then I'll move into the** (**crawlspace** or **basement**, as applicable), **then up to the attic, and then finally to the interior."**

"As I inspect each area, I'll check one of these boxes." Show Lot & Landscaping section, and point to boxes. **"If I check the no problem box, then of course there's no problem; if I check the minimal box, then that means that its something easy to fix, and may not even cost any money. If I check the minor box, that means that it may cost a significant amount to fix it, say on the order of a few hundred dollars or so; and if I check the Major box, then that means a major problem that will cost a lot of money, like a new roof or a new heating system. Or,**

it could mean a safety item that requires immediate attention."

Then say: **"And when I check one of these three boxes** (point to minimal, minor, major boxes on page)**, I'll go down here** (point to comment section) **and write down exactly what I mean. Then, after the inspection is complete, we'll sit down and go over each comment in detail."**

You are now ready for the inspection agreement. Recommended procedures for presenting this agreement are covered in the next section.

4.4 THE INSPECTION AGREEMENT

This section details the recommended procedures for presenting and signing the Home Inspection Agreement. A sample agreement is shown on the next page.

Put the blank, bound report down or place it below your clipboard. Then say: **"The last thing I have is the Home Inspection Agreement."** Show the agreement to your client; it should be at the top of your clipboard. **"It comes in two parts, of which you'll get a copy."** Lift the first page to show the yellow copy to client. While pointing to the words on the agreement, you say: **"This agreement says that me, the inspector, will inspect this property for the sum of** (state amount)**."** Looking at client, say **"That means there are no hidden charges."** Looking back down and pointing to the words in the agreement, say **"The inspectee, who is you, shall make payment in full prior to the delivery of the inspection report. That means that you will pay me when I'm finished**

```
(Your company name,
address, and telephone
  number goes here)
```

Date: _____

HOME INSPECTION AGREEMENT

1. **The INSPECTOR shall inspect the property located at:**

    Address: _____

    City/County: _____ **State:** _____

    for the sum of $_____**. The INSPECTEE shall make payment
    in full prior to delivery of the Inspection Report.**

2. **The inspection will consist of a two to three hour visual
    inspection of all readily accessible areas of the dwelling
    and property. No destructive testing will be performed.**

3. **The INSPECTEE hereby agrees that the INSPECTOR shall not be
    held liable in any way for any past, present, or future
    defects in material or workmanship on the subject property,
    or for any errors or omissions in the inspection, or for any
    other consequences of the inspection.**

INSPECTOR SIGNATURE _____ **Date** _____

INSPECTEE SIGNATURE _____ **Date** _____

Copyright 1994, Pompeii Engineers

here today, after I give you the completed report."

Continuing on and pointing to the words, you say: **"The second paragraph says that this is a two to three hour visual inspection of all readily accessible areas of the dwelling and property, and that no destructive testing will be performed."** Looking back up at the client, say: **"That means that I will check only what I can see. For example, if there's a hole in a wall and its covered by a picture or a couch, I won't find it because I won't move the picture or the couch. Or, if I have to cut a hole in a wall or remove ductwork to get a closer look, I won't do it because I can't destroy or alter any piece of the property. Instead, I'll just state that that area should be further investigated."**

Pointing down at the words again, you say: **"The third paragraph is a general release of liability for me. It says that the inspector shall not be held liable in any way for any past, present, or future defects in the subject property, for any errors or omissions in the inspection, or for any other consequences of the inspection."** Looking back up at client, you say: **"This means that there are no guarantees because this is just a two to three hour visual inspection."**

Most clients will not ask anything else about the agreement and will be ready to sign it. However, some clients may question the release of liability or "no guarantee" statement in one way or another. If they do, your response is: **"This is just a two to three hour visual inspection, and any home inspector will not give a guarantee for this type of inspection. For me to provide a guarantee, I would have to spend anywhere from 40 to 60 hours here and would need permission to do destructive testing, such as cutting holes in walls."** If the client asks what you would charge for this guarantee, just

52

tell them your standard fee is $75 dollars per hour for 40 to 60 hours. They will quickly realize that its not worth the extra cost.

When you have answered any questions about the agreement, you say: **"Now I'll sign and date this** (while you are signing it) **and then give it to you for signature."** Give the clipboard to the client for their signature. After their signature, you say: **"Okay, we can go ahead and get started."** You now proceed back to the vehicle, remove the top (white) section of the agreement, and put that copy, along with your license and any extra business cards you may have, back into your briefcase.

Next, place a blank report in your clipboard with the Lot & Landscaping page at the top. If you use two-part NCR forms, remember to place a solid item (such as the cardboard backing from a tablet) below the top pages to prevent writing through the pressure sensitive NCR forms. If you use just plain paper copies of the report, the cardboard backer is not needed.

There has been considerable debate whether or not the inspector needs to keep a copy of the entire report for his or her records. It's nice for the inspector to have a complete copy for his/her records, but may not be absolutely necessary. If any problems or litigation over a particular inspection should happen to come up at a later date, it is the responsibility of the person with the report to provide you with a copy in order to substantiate their claim. Therefore, the decision to use plain paper copies of the report or two-part NCR copies of the report should be based on the comfort level of the inspector, and possibly the advice of a competent lawyer.

Strap on your toolbelt; you are now ready to start the inspection

CHAPTER 5: INSPECTING AND REPORTING

5.1 INSPECTION SAFETY

There are many safety hazards that can be encountered during the course of a home inspection. You must ALWAYS exercise caution and must ALWAYS be constantly aware of safety hazards when performing inspections. If you are ever in doubt about the safety of any part of any inspection- SKIP THAT PART OF THE INSPECTION. Explain on your report and to the client that the inspection of that particular item or area may present a safety hazard to the inspector.

Some common rules that you or your inspectors must follow include:

1) <u>Beware of roofs</u>. Never go on top of a roof during the course of a routine inspection. There is too much of a chance that you could slip and fall, or that a part of the subroof is rotted or missing, causing you to fall through the roof. Always inspect roofs from the ground with your binoculars. If for some reason you absolutely must walk on a roof, ensure that the roof is not pitched too steeply and that you have completely checked the subroofing in the attic area for rotted or missing boards. Warning-- roofs made of somewhat brittle materials, such as wood shakes or slate, may crack if you walk on them. If you crack them, you will probably be made responsible for fixing them!

2) <u>Beware of electrical shock hazards</u>. Exercise extreme caution around all electrical circuit

panels, wiring, junction boxes, switches, and outlets. NEVER assume that an circuit or outlet is wired correctly; you never know who wired it. NEVER assume that the black is the hot wire, the white is neutral, and the green is ground. They may be switched!!!

3) <u>Beware of crawlspace hazards</u>. Do not enter any area of the crawlspace where you cannot easily crawl on your hands and knees. Keep a sharp eye out for spiders (black widow and brown recluse), snakes, or other animals. The screwdriver in your hand can also double as a defensive weapon. Always try to get as much light as possible into the crawlspace, and always use your more powerful lantern flashlight. If you see a purple colored tint or any powder-like material on the crawlspace floor, stay away from it- it's probably some type of insecticide (or maybe rodent urine!). Watch out for loose electrical wiring; it could be energized, and you may get shocked because you are in contact with the wire and the possibly wet ground. If you are ever in doubt about your safety in entering a crawlspace- DO NOT ENTER THE CRAWLSPACE. Just write in your report and explain to your client that this area was not accessible because you deemed it a safety hazard. Write the reason why you deemed the area a safety hazard.

4) <u>Beware of attic hazards</u>. The greatest attic hazard is falling through the ceiling due to a poorly supported or non-existent attic floor. Many houses use prefabricated 2 x 4 trusses in their attic areas with no flooring, forcing you to "walk" only on the trusses themselves. If you miss a truss, your weight will put you right through the ceiling in the room below. Never crawl in an attic of this type. Use your own judgement on how far you can enter any attic area; each house will be different.

5) <u>Use caution when using ladders</u>. Never go above one story in height (about 10 feet) when using a ladder during an inspection. Use your binoculars instead. Also be careful

when using a ladder to enter attic areas. If you are agile, your six foot step ladder may be high enough to get you into an attic hatch in a house with 8 foot ceilings. If you are not agile or if the ceilings are higher than 8 feet, you may need to use a 7 or 8 foot stepladder, or maybe even your 16 foot extension ladder. Whatever you do, don't take any chances.

6) <u>Beware of lead paint and asbestos hazards</u>. If you are in an older home, be aware any flaking paint may possibly contain lead. Be careful not to stir up any dust in these areas to keep from inhaling any small, airborne lead particles. Also be careful around any old pipe insulation, old sheet flooring, ceiling tiles, roof tiles, or any other material that may contain asbestos. Be careful not to stir up any dust in these areas to keep from inhaling any airborne asbestos particles.

This is only a partial listing of the many hazards to your safety that you may encounter during the course of your home inspections. Remember- every house is different and every house will present its own unique hazards to you. You must always use your own best judgement in every situation. Above all, ALWAYS BE AWARE OF YOUR SURROUNDINGS and NEVER TAKE ANY CHANCES.

5.2 THE HOME INSPECTION REPORT

Included in the following pages is a sample of the Pompeii Home Inspection Report. This report provides the framework for the detailed home inspection method used in this book. This report is highly recommended because it provides a relatively simple, logical, and methodical approach to use when inspecting a home. It also helps you, the inspector, to not miss anything during the inspection by prompting you with a checklist type format to help ensure coverage of each item in a specific area of the inspection.

This copyrighted report is available for use in your business. Interested persons can purchase a blank set of forms that comes with a non-transferable Copyright License that allows the inspector to make unlimited copies for his or her company's use. All you need to do is to add your company letterhead, make copies, then start inspecting. A Home Inspection Agreement is included with each report. Specific ordering information can be found in Appendix B of this book.

This reporting system is highly recommended to minimize your legal risk and to help you perform a high quality, thorough inspection.

5.3 INSPECTION REPORTING

There are some specific rules that you should follow when inspecting houses or buildings and for filling out the Pompeii Home Inspection Report (or similar). These rules are:

1) <u>Always use a high quality pen with black ink</u>. Pencils must not be used because your report can be changed by others too easily. If you make a mistake, just draw a line through it and initial it. Or, you can just get a new sheet.

2) <u>Always print in uppercase block letters only</u>. These letters are easiest to read and understand. Cursive writing or printing with lowercase letters vary too much from person to person, and may be hard for readers to decipher.

3) <u>Always print neatly and clearly</u>. This is an absolute must! If you cannot print neatly and clearly, then you must practice and learn to print neatly and clearly. There is nothing less professional in appearance than a report with scribbles and messy printing. If you determine that you will not be able to print clearly, you may want to consider using a software-based report.

4) <u>Write what you observed, then write any opinion or recommendation you may have</u>. Reporting this way will help others to better understand your report and will help keep you out of legal trouble. For example, if you see a crack in a basement slab, you might write "CRACK OBSERVED IN SOUTHWEST CORNER OF SLAB. NOT STRUCTURALLY SIGNIFICANT AT THIS TIME. RECOMMEND MONITOR OVER NEXT YEAR FOR ADDITIONAL MOVEMENT."

5) <u>Always refer to specialists if further inspection is necessary</u>. When you find something that you feel should be more thoroughly inspected or checked out, shift the "inspection burden" to someone who specializes in that particular area, like an HVAC technician, electrician, chimney sweep, etc. This will also help to keep you out of legal trouble, spend less time taking things apart, and allow you to more efficiently spend your time on other areas of the inspection. For example, you might write: "SOME CREOSOTE BUILDUP OBSERVED IN FLUE. RECOMMEND COMPLETE CHECKOUT AND CLEANING BY QUALIFIED CHIMNEY SWEEP BEFORE FIRING."

6) <u>Always write down areas that are not accessible or only partly accessible</u>. This will help reduce any confusion over what you inspected and did not inspect, and will also help to avoid legal problems. Write "NOT ACCESSIBLE" or "PARTIALLY ACCESSIBLE" in the space immediately to the right of the item. You could write the reason in the comment section. For example: "FOUNDATION WALLS ONLY PARTLY ACCESSIBLE DUE TO INSULATION COVERING."

7) <u>Always write down areas not inspected due to safety hazards</u>. You must never inspect anything that you feel may cause significant risk of injury to you. Just write it down. For example, you could write: "ATTIC AREA NOT ACCESSIBLE DUE TO OPEN WIRING ACROSS ACCESS HATCH."

8) <u>Always rely on the written report, and not the verbal report</u>. You must always assume that your client will forget everything you told them during the inspection. Only what is written will be preserved after you leave the site, and only what is written will be available for judges to review in court. You are helping to protect yourself from legal trouble by relying solely on your written report.

9) <u>Always keep your comments brief and to the point</u>. The best way to report on the condition of an item is to keep it clear and concise. The more you write, the more confusing the item generally becomes, and the less time you have to properly inspect other parts of the house.

10) <u>Always recommend immediate repair of possible hazards</u>. If there is anything that could cause a significant hazard to any people in or around the house, recommend that it be repaired immediately. This helps to prevent any litigation against you if anyone should

60

be injured in the future. Examples are trip hazards, open wiring, dead trees, holes in floors, open plumbing vents, loose boards, missing railings, poor flue venting, etc.

Other instructions for filling out the report:

If a particular item on your inspection checklist does not apply to the house you are inspecting, just write "NA" (which means Not Applicable) in the "No problem" box. For example, if the house does not have a garage, write "NA" on that line. Make sure you explain this to your client during the verbal presentation.

If a particular item is not accessible, just write a dash "-" in the "No Problem" box, and write "NOT ACCESSIBLE" directly beside the item.

Use a code system to assign an "Inspection #" for each inspection. A good code system is "YMMDDA", where Y is the year (i.e., "1" for 2001), MM is the number of the month (i.e., "12" for December), DD is the day (i.e., "20" for December 20th), and A is for the order for inspections that day (i.e., "A" for the first inspection of that day, "B" for the second inspection, and "C" for the third inspection). As an example, the specific inspection number for the first inspection that day would be 11220A. This code MUST be placed on every sheet of the Home Inspection Report.

A trick of the trade for determining the age of most houses is in the toilet tank. Every toilet has their date of manufacture stamped into the ceramic tank or tank cover. Just lift the cover up while you are checking the toilet, and look for the date. This will work on most houses that have not had their toilets replaced. Or, for very old houses, it will give you a good idea when the bathroom was last remodeled.

61

The sample report follows. Each page has been completed with a sample inspection to show you a good method for filling out the report. You can fill out your reports using the same method and the same type of wording.

[Your company name,
address, and phone
number goes here]

Home Inspection Report

Date __12/20/97__

HOME INSPECTION REPORT

Inspection # __71220B__

Inspection Address __519 W. WASHINGTON AVENUE__

City __ANYTOWN__   State __VA__

Name __JOHN HOMEBUYER__

Mailing Address __3251 W. 30TH ST.__

City __ANYTOWN__   State __VA__   Zip __22123__

Phone __(540) 555-3121__

Home Description __RAMBLER OVER FULL WALKOUT BASEMENT__
__WITH ATTACHED TWO CAR GARAGE.__

Approx. Age of Home __12 YEARS__

Date of Last Significant Rainfall __12/10/97__

Inspector Signature __Joe Inspector__   JOE INSPECTOR

Number of pages in this report __16__

Copyright ©1994 Pompeii Engineers

I T E M #	Home Inspection Report ⊕POMPEII REPORTS LOT & LANDSCAPING INSPECTION # 71220 B	NO PROBLEM	MINIMAL	MINOR	MAJOR
1	Storm water runoff			✓	
2	Foundation grading	✓			
3	Low spots/standing water	✓			
4	Overhanging trees		✓		
5	Trees/shrubs condition	✓			
6	Grass/lawn condition	✓			
7	Driveway condition ASPHALT	✓			
8	Sidewalk/walkway condition	✓			
9	Garage condition		✓		
10	Storage shed/outbuildings	NA			
11	Outdoor lighting	✓			

COMMENTS: ① ADD EXTENSION TO FRONT RIGHT AND REAR
RIGHT DOWNSPOUTS TO DEPOSIT WATER AT LEAST 7 FEET
FROM FOUNDATION.

① POOR GRADING OF REAR YARD OBSERVED. RECOMMEND
ADD SWALE TO DIRECT WATER INTO NORTH CULVERT.

④ HOUSE WITHIN FALL RADIUS OF SEVERAL LARGE TREES.
RECOMMEND MONITOR TREE HEALTH.

⑨ LARGE GAP AT BOTTOM OF RIGHT DOOR WHEN CLOSED.

Copyright ©1994 Pompeii Engineers

I T E M #	Home Inspection Report POMPEII REPORTS EXTERIOR INSPECTION # 71220B	N O P R O B L E M	M I N I M A L	M I N O R	M A J O R
1	Siding condition VINYL	✓			
2	Siding properly installed		✓		
3	Exterior trim condition			✓	
4	Adequate caulking	✓			
5	Ground contact with wood	✓			
6	Mildew present	✓			
7	Condition of doors/windows	✓			
8	Front porch condition		✓		
9	Deck/patio condition		✓		
10	Exterior steps condition	✓			
11	Exterior electrical receptacles GFI	✓			
12	Exterior plumbing fixtures	✓			

COMMENTS: (2) LOOSE SIDING OBSERVED AT LOWER RIGHT
FRONT. REPAIR.

(3) ROTTED TRIM BOARDS AT LOWER SOUTHEAST CORNER,
LOWER SOUTHWEST CORNER, AND AROUND MANY WINDOWS.
REPAIR.

(8) PORCH RAILING LOOSE. REPAIR.

(9) DECK ATTACHED TO HOUSE WITH ONLY NAILS. RECOMMEND
USE LAG BOLTS FOR ADDED SUPPORT.

Copyright ©1994 Pompeii Engineers

I T E M #	Home Inspection Report ⊕ POMPEII REPORTS ROOFING INSPECTION # 71220B	N O P R O B L E M	M I N I M A L	M I N O R	M A J O R
1	Roofing material condition	✓			
2	Roofing properly installed	✓			
3	Missing shingles		✓		
4	Shingle blisters/curled edges	✓			
5	Roof moss/mildew	✓			
6	Flashing condition		✓		
7	Cracks/gaps in roofing		✓		
8	Evidence of leaks	✓			
9	Skylights watertight	✓			
10	Gutter/downspout condition		✓		

COMMENTS: ③ SHINGLE TABS (3 TOTAL) MISSING FROM NORTHEAST SECTION OF ROOF. REPAIR.

⑥⑦ GAP OBSERVED IN ATTIC AREA AROUND CHIMNEY. REPAIR TO PREVENT LEAKAGE.

⑩ MOST GUTTERS CLOGGED WITH LEAVES. RECOMMEND CLEANING.

⑩ MISSING DOWNSPOUT ELBOWS AT NORTH AND WEST CORNERS. REPLACE.

Copyright © 1994 Pompeii Engineers

ITEM #	Home Inspection Report POMPEII REPORTS	NO PROBLEM	MINIMAL	MINOR	MAJOR
	FOUNDATION INSPECTION # 71220B				
1	Foundation material & workmanship	✓			
2	Foundation mortar deteriorating	✓			
3	Settling: Cracks in walls		✓		
4	Settling: Cracks in slab	✓			
5	Settling: Slab level	✓			
6	Settling: Roof/Wall deflections	✓			
7	Moisture: Water marks		✓		
8	Moisture: Fungus/mildew growth	✓			
9	Moisture: Musty odor	✓			
10	Basement floor drain	✓			
11	Crawlspace ventilation	NA			
12	Crawlspace vapor barrier	NA			

COMMENTS: NOTE: FOUNDATION WALLS NOT TOTALLY ACCESSIBLE DUE TO FINISHED BASEMENT.

③ SEVERAL SMALL CRACKS OBSERVED IN SOUTH WALL DUE TO NORMAL CONCRETE SHRINKAGE. NOT STRUCTURALLY SIGNIFICANT.

⑦ EFFLORESCENCE OBSERVED AT INTERIOR FOUNDATION WALL, SOUTHWEST CORNER. PROBABLE CAUSE IS POOR EXTERIOR DRAINAGE. SEE "EXTERIOR" SECTION.

Copyright © 1994 Pompeii Engineers

I T E M #	Home Inspection Report ⊕ **POMPEII** REPORTS _FRAMING_ INSPECTION # 71220B	N O P R O B L E M	M I N I M A L	M I N O R	M A J O R
1	Main beam condition	✓			
2	Floor joist size/type 2×10 16"o.c.	✓			
3	Floor joist deflection	✓			
4	Subflooring size/type 23/32"	✓			
5	Subflooring deflection	✓			
6	Wall stud size/type MOST WALLS NOT ACCESSIBLE	✓			
7	Wall stud deflection	✓			
8	Roof rafter/truss size/type	✓			
9	Roof rafter/truss deflection		✓		
10	Roof sheathing size/type 7/16"	✓			
11	Roof sheathing deflection	✓			
12	Framing dry and firm	✓			

COMMENTS: ⑨ SLIGHT DEFLECTION OBSERVED IN RIDGE
BEAM. NOT STRUCTURALLY SIGNIFICANT.

_____

_____

_____

_____

_____

_____

_____

_____

Copyright ©1994 Pompeii Engineers

I T E M #	Home Inspection Report POMPEII REPORTS INSULATION INSPECTION # 71220 B	NO PROBLEM	MINIMAL	MINOR	MAJOR
1	Attic insulation: R = 19 BLOWN CELLULOSE			✓	
2	Attic hatch insulation	✓			
3	Attic ventilation adequate	✓			
4	Wall insulation: R = ~11+ NOT ACCESSIBLE	✓			
5	Floor/crawlspace insulation: R = 19		✓		
6	Evidence of vapor barrier problems	✓			
7	Double/triple pane windows	✓			
8	Door/window weatherstripping	✓			

COMMENTS: ① R-19 IS NOT RECOMMENDED FOR THIS AREA. RECOMMEND UPGRADE TO R-30.

⑤ MISSING OR LOOSE BATTS OBSERVED IN BASEMENT AREA. REPAIR.

Copyright ©1994 Pompeii Engineers

ITEM #	Home Inspection Report POMPEII REPORTS ELECTRICAL INSPECTION # 71220B	NO PROBLEM	MINIMAL	MINOR	MAJOR
1	Amp service adequate 200 AMP	✓			
2	Adequate number of circuits	✓			
3	Main circuit panel condition	✓			
4	Circuits labeled PARTIAL		✓		
5	Fuses/breakers adequate			✓	
6	20+ amp circuit for kitchen	✓			
7	20+ amp circuit for laundry	✓			
8	30+ amp circuit for heat/AC	✓			
9	30+ amp circuit for hot water	✓			
10	Exterior service condition	✓			
11	Receptacle condition		✓		
12	Receptacles properly grounded		✓		

COMMENTS: ⑤ UNDERSIZED WIRES AND/OR OVERSIZED FUSES
OBSERVED INSIDE MAIN PANEL. RECOMMEND IMMEDIATE
INSPECTION AND CORRECTION BY QUALIFIED ELECTRICIAN.
⑪ NUMEROUS RECEPTACLES LOOSE AND REQUIRE SECURING.
⑪ OPEN JUNCTION BOX AT BASEMENT CEILING. REPAIR.
⑫ HOT/NEUTRAL WIRES REVERSED AT ALL GARAGE
RECEPTACLES. REPAIR.

Copyright ©1994 Pompeii Engineers

I T E M #	Home Inspection Report 🌐 POMPEII REPORTS PLUMBING INSPECTION # 71220B	N O P R O B L E M	M I N I M A L	M I N O R	M A J O R
1	Water supply pressure/flow rate	✓			
2	Water supply piping size/material	✓			
3	Water supply shut-off valve	✓			
4	Dielectric couplings	✓			
5	Water hammer problem	✓			
6	Evidence of supply leaks		✓		
7	Kitchen/Bath sink shut-off valves	✓			
8	Drain piping size/material	✓			
9	Drainage rate adequate	✓			
10	Drain traps in place	✓			
11	Drain venting adequate	✓			
12	Evidence of sewer backup problem NONE VISIBLE	✓			
13	Hot water heater capacity 50 GALLONS	✓			
14	Hot water heater condition				✓

COMMENTS: ⑥ OLD WATER STAINS ON BASEMENT CEILING
TILES INDICATE PAST LEAKAGE. RECOMMEND ASK
HOMEOWNER ABOUT HISTORY OF LEAK.
⑭ DANGER! NO PRESSURE- TEMPERATURE RELIEF VALVE
INSTALLED. RECOMMEND IMMEDIATE REPAIR BY QUALIFIED
PLUMBER.

Copyright ©1994 Pompeii Engineers

ITEM #	Home Inspection Report 🌐 POMPEII REPORTS HEATING / COOLING INSPECTION # 71220B	NO PROBLEM	MINIMAL	MINOR	MAJOR
1	System type: GAS FURNACE / CENTRAL A/C	✓			
2	Estimate of heating/cooling efficiency	—			
3	Compressor unit condition	✓			
4	Compressed freon line insulated	✓			
5	Compressor unit level & ventilated		✓		
6	Interior unit/furnace condition	✓	.		
7	Combustion air availability	✓			
8	Condensate drain present	✓			
9	Air filter maintenance		✓		
10	Ductwork size/material	✓			
11	Thermostat condition	✓			
12	(Gas)/Oil service line		✓		

COMMENTS: ② A/C NOT TESTED DUE TO LOW OUTSIDE AIR
TEMPERATURE OF 45°F.

⑤ OUTSIDE UNIT NOT LEVEL. REPAIR.

⑨ FILTER DIRTY. REPLACE.

⑫ NATURAL GAS SUPPLY LINE IS POORLY SUPPORTED
IN BASEMENT CEILING AREA. RECOMMEND ADD ADDITIONAL
SUPPORTS.

Copyright © 1994 Pompeii Engineers

I T E M #	Home Inspection Report POMPEII REPORTS BATHROOM # 1 HALL BATH INSPECTION # 71220B	NO PROBLEM	MINIMAL	MINOR	MAJOR
1	Bathroom layout	✓			
2	Bathroom sink condition	✓			
3	Evidence of water leakage	✓			
4	Bathtub/shower condition	✓			
5	Water-resistant surfaces		✓		
6	Toilet condition		✓		
7	Bathroom ventilation FAN	✓			
8	Bathroom electrical receptacles		✓		
9	Bathroom lighting	✓			
10	Sufficient heating	✓			

COMMENTS: ⑤ CAULK AT LOWER TUB EDGE TO PREVENT WATER INFILTRATION.

⑥ INNER BOWL STAINED AND DISCOLORED.

⑧ NO GFI.

Copyright © 1994 Pompeii Engineers

ITEM #	Home Inspection Report POMPEII REPORTS KITCHEN INSPECTION # 71220B	NO PROBLEM	MINIMAL	MINOR	MAJOR
1	Kitchen layout	✓			
2	Cabinet condition	✓			
3	Countertop condition		✓		
4	Kitchen sink condition	✓			
5	Evidence of water leakage	✓			
6	Garbage disposal condition		✓		
7	Stove/range condition		✓		
8	Range hood/vent	✓			
9	Refrigerator condition	✓			
10	Dishwasher condition	✓			
11	Kitchen lighting	✓			
12	Electrical receptacles NO GFI		✓		

COMMENTS: ③ LARGE CHIPS OBSERVED IN SEVERAL LOCATIONS.

⑥ DISPOSAL APPEARS JAMMED; RECOMMEND REPAIR

  BY QUALIFIED PLUMBER.

⑦ RIGHT REAR BURNER INOPERABLE.

Copyright © 1994 Pompeii Engineers

ITEM #	Home Inspection Report 🌐 POMPEII REPORTS INTERIOR INSPECTION # 71220B	NO PROBLEM	MINIMAL	MINOR	MAJOR
1	Wall condition		✓		
2	Ceiling condition		✓		
3	Flooring/carpeting condition			✓	
4	Moulding & trim	✓			
5	Interior doors		✓		
6	Condition of windows	✓			
7	Presence of odors	✓			
8	Attic access HATCH	✓			
9	Lighting	✓			
10	Closet space	✓			

COMMENTS: ① ② MINOR COSMETIC DRYWALL CRACKS AND
NAIL POPS OBSERVED THROUGHOUT.

③ LIVING ROOM CARPET WORN.

⑤ NORTHEAST BEDROOM DOOR DOES NOT LATCH PROPERLY.
REPAIR.

Copyright ©1994 Pompeii Engineers

ITEM #	Home Inspection Report POMPEII REPORTS SAFETY INSPECTION # 71220B	NO PROBLEM	MINIMAL	MINOR	MAJOR
1	Bedroom fire escapes		✓		
2	Smoke detectors installed		✓		
3	Exterior door deadbolts	✓			
4	Window latches/locks	✓			
5	GFI circuit in bathrooms NONE		✓		
6	GFI circuit in kitchen NONE		✓		
7	GFI circuit for exterior NONE		✓		
8	Exterior stair railings	✓			
9	Interior stair railings	✓			
10	Hot water heater venting	NA			
11	Furnace venting SEE BELOW	✓			
12	Fireplace condition	✓			
13	Woodstove condition/placement	NA			
14	Chimney/flue condition NOT TOTALLY ACCESSIBLE	✓			
15	Lead Paint Test (extra)	NA			
16	Radon Test (extra) NOT TESTED			✓	

COMMENTS: ① ALL BEDROOMS AT UPPER LEVEL; NO ESCAPE LADDERS PRESENT.

② NO SMOKE DETECTOR AT LOWER LEVEL. INSTALL.

⑪ STRONGLY RECOMMEND INSTALL CARBON MONOXIDE DETECTOR(S).

⑯ RECOMMEND RADON SCREENING TO DETERMINE IF RADON HAZARD IS PRESENT.

Copyright © 1994 Pompeii Engineers

CONTINUATION PAGE

SECTION: _____   INSPECTION # _____

COMMENTS: (continued from previous page)

_____

_____

_____

_____

_____

_____

_____

_____

_____

_____

_____

_____

_____

_____

_____

_____

_____

_____

_____

_____

Copyright 1996 Pompeii Engineers

CHAPTER 6: INSPECTION PROCEDURES

This chapter provides detailed procedures for inspecting a home and filling out the Pompeii Home Inspection Report (or similar) shown in Chapter 5. Each of the following sections explains how to complete each page of the report in an easy to use, step-by-step format.

6.1 LOT & LANDSCAPING

This section describes the procedure to use for inspecting the Lot & Landscaping. The required Lot & Landscaping inspection sheet can be found in Chapter 5 for you to follow and help guide you through the inspection. Each numbered item listed below corresponds to the numbered item on the inspection sheet.

1. <u>Storm water runoff</u>. This is one of the most important items of the entire inspection. How rain water flows and drains around the house will determine if the house is prone to water problems. You must look at the way the house sits on the lot, where downspouts deposit water, and the slope of the land around the house. Some common comments that you may use include:

"ADD EXTENSION TO FRONT RIGHT AND REAR RIGHT DOWNSPOUTS TO DEPOSIT WATER AT LEAST 6 FEET FROM FOUNDATION."

"POOR GRADING OF REAR YARD OBSERVED. RECOMMEND ADD SWALE TO DIRECT WATER INTO NORTH CULVERT."

"POOR DRAINAGE OBSERVED AT AREA JUST TO LEFT OF GARAGE DOOR. RECOMMEND ADD SURFACE DRAIN AND DEPOSIT WATER AT FRONT CULVERT."

2. Foundation grading. Make sure the grading around the foundation slopes away from the foundation. Most homes are properly graded around the foundation when new, but the backfill almost always sinks a few inches over the first few years. One common comment:

"REVERSE SLOPE OBSERVED AT REAR AND RIGHT SIDES. RECOMMEND ADD BACKFILL TO DIRECT WATER AWAY FROM FOUNDATION."

3. Low spots/standing water. Look over the lot for any low spots or standing water. One common comment:

"SEVERAL LOW SPOTS OBSERVED ON EAST SIDE OF LOT. RECOMMEND FILL WITH TOPSOIL TO LEVEL."

4. Overhanging trees. Scan the areas next to the house for any trees that could possibly fall and damage the house. You should especially look for any large trees that are dead or dying. Some common comments:

"HOUSE WITHIN FALL RADIUS OF SEVERAL LARGE TREES.

80

RECOMMEND MONITOR TREE HEALTH."

"LARGE DEAD TREE OBSERVED IN NORTH CORNER OF LOT. RECOMMEND IMMEDIATE REMOVAL TO PREVENT DAMAGE OR INJURY."

5. Trees/shrubs condition. Look at general overall condition of trees and shrubs. Don't spend a lot of time looking at each individual tree or shrub; just give a quick assessment to conserve your time for more important areas. Make sure that no trees or shrubs are touching the house. This acts like a 'mulch' and draws moisture (and subsequent rot) and insects to those areas. Some common comments:

"TWO DEAD SHRUBS OBSERVED IN FRONT YARD."

"TRIM BACK SHRUBS TO PREVENT TOUCHING HOUSE."

6. Grass/lawn condition. Report on your first impression of the lawn. Don't be too picky here and don't get into much detail. Some common comments:

"POOR GRASS GROWTH IN FRONT."

"LAWN NEEDS MAINTENANCE."

7. Driveway condition. Look for any ruts, potholes, cracking, etc. List the type of driveway (gravel, asphalt, concrete, etc.) up beside the item. Remember that driveways are for convenience only, and any cracks or flaws that do not affect the stability of the house itself are cosmetic only, unless they present a safety hazard. Some common comments:

"RUTS OBSERVED. RECOMMEND ADD MORE GRAVEL TO FILL MUDDY AREAS."

"POTHOLES OBSERVED. RECOMMEND FILLING & PATCHING."

"ASPHALT DETERIORATION OBSERVED. CRACK TYPES INDICATE POSSIBLE SHORT REMAINING LIFE."

"SOME CRACKS OBSERVED IN CONCRETE. RECOMMEND FILL CRACKS WITH MASONRY CAULK TO PREVENT WATER INFILTRATION."

"NUMEROUS CRACKS OBSERVED IN CONCRETE. CRACK TYPES INDICATE POSSIBLE IMPROPER CURING, IMPROPER MIX, IMPROPER BASE, OR IMPROPER SLAB DEPTH."

8. Sidewalk/walkway condition. Check the general condition of sidewalk. Look specifically for any trip hazards. A common comment:

"LIFTED SLAB PRESENTS A TRIP HAZARD. RECOMMEND IMMEDIATE REPAIR."

9. Garage condition. Check the construction of the garage, the opening and closing of garage doors, garage door hardware, any automatic openers, the slab, the direction the slab drains, the fireproofing installed if an attached garage, and the presence and possible hazard of any fuel burning appliance (hot water heater, furnace, etc.) at the garage slab level. Some common comments:

"LARGE GAP AT BOTTOM OF RIGHT DOOR WHEN CLOSED."

"AUTOMATIC OPENER VERY NOISY."

10. <u>Storage shed/outbuildings</u>. Take a quick look at any storage sheds or other outbuildings. Just provide a general assessment. If the outbuilding is too large to inspect in just a few minutes, state that it is a building in itself and requires a separate inspection. A common comment:

"SHED IN GENERALLY POOR CONDITION."

11. <u>Outdoor lighting</u>. The house should have at least one exterior light at each exterior door. Larger lots in more remote areas should have larger floodlights for security purposes. Some common comments:

"REAR LIGHT INOPERABLE (BULB?)."

"POOR LIGHTING IN DRIVEWAY AREA. RECOMMEND ADD LIGHTING FOR SECURITY PURPOSES."

6.2 EXTERIOR

This section describes the procedure to use for inspecting the Exterior. The required Exterior inspection sheet can be found in Chapter 5 for you to follow and help guide you through the inspection. Each numbered item listed below corresponds to the numbered item on the inspection sheet.

1. <u>Siding condition</u>. Check the condition of all exposed siding. List the siding type beside the item (wood, vinyl, aluminum, stucco, etc.). Look for any missing pieces of siding. Some common comments:

"SIGNIFICANT DIRT AND MILDEW OBSERVED ON VINYL SIDING. RECOMMEND CLEANING WITH PRESSURE WASHER."

"BLISTERING AND PEELING OF PAINT OBSERVED ON WOOD SIDING. RECOMMEND SCRAPE, CLEAN, CAULK, AND PAINT."

"ALUMINUM (or vinyl) SIDING WAVY AND UNEVEN INDICATES POOR QUALITY AND/OR IMPROPER INSTALLATION."

"3 FOOT SECTION MISSING AT UPPER RIGHT SIDE NEAR GABLE."

2. <u>Siding properly installed</u>. Check to see if the siding is properly installed. If vinyl or aluminum siding, slide a few pieces in their slots to make sure the nails are floated and not set tight. Check if the siding meets with the trim (J-channels) properly, and that it is tucked in properly. Some common comments:

"LOOSE SIDING OBSERVED AT LOWER RIGHT FRONT. REPAIR."

"POOR CUTTING AND FITTING OF J-CHANNEL OBSERVED."

84

3. Exterior trim condition. Check all visible trim, including soffit and fascia. Some common comments:

"PAINT PEELING AT SOFFIT AND FASCIA. RECOMMEND SCRAPE, CLEAN, AND RE-PAINT."

"ROTTED TRIM BOARDS AT LOWER SOUTHEAST CORNER, LOWER SOUTHWEST CORNER, AND AROUND MANY WINDOWS. REPAIR."

4. Adequate caulking. Look around all windows, doors, and where dissimilar materials or trim pieces meet for cracked or missing caulking. Don't go into great detail for every single window or door; just keep it general. A common comment:

"SOME CRACKED CAULKING AROUND WINDOWS AND DOORS. RECOMMEND REMOVE OLD CAULK AND RE-CAULK AFFECTED AREAS."

5. Ground contact with wood. Make sure that no wood or wood trim pieces are in direct contact with the ground. This invites rot and insects. A common comment:

"TRIM BOARD AT FRONT RIGHT LOWER CORNER CONTACTING GROUND. CUT BOARD OR RE-GRADE."

6. Mildew present. Check for any significant mildew growth on siding or trim, especially north facing siding and soffitt boards (no sun). A common comment:

"MODERATE MILDEW BUILDUP AT NORTH SIDE SOFFITT.

RECOMMEND CLEAN AND KILL MILDEW WITH BLEACH SOLUTION."

7. Condition of doors/windows. Look for any deficiencies on doors and windows from the outside. Also check for any cracked windows or broken trim pieces. A common comment:

"BROKEN WINDOWS AT REAR AND LEFT SIDE (4 TOTAL)."

8. Front porch condition. Check the structural stability and construction of front porch and steps (if any). Some common comments:

"CRACK OBSERVED BETWEEN PORCH AND STEPS. RECOMMEND FILL WITH MASONRY CAULK TO PREVENT WATER INFILTRATION."

"ROTTED BOARDS AT PORCH FLOOR. REPAIR."

"PORCH RAILING LOOSE. REPAIR."

"MISSING BALUSTERS AT RAILING. REPAIR."

9. Deck/patio condition. Check the structural stability and construction of the deck and/or patio (if any). Some common comments:

"DECK ATTACHED TO HOUSE WITH ONLY NAILS. RECOMMEND USE LAG BOLTS FOR ADDED SUPPORT."

"SEVERAL SPLIT/MISSING BOARDS AT DECK FLOOR. REPAIR."

"PATIO SLAB NOT LEVEL DUE TO SETTLING."

"DECK RAILING PARTIALLY LOOSE. REPAIR."

"PATIO SLAB IMPROPERLY SLOPED TOWARD HOUSE. RECOMMEND REPAIR TO SLOPE AWAY FROM HOUSE."

"DECK SAGS IN CENTER DUE TO OVERSPAN OF JOISTS. RECOMMEND REPAIR IMMEDIATELY."

10. Exterior steps condition. Check the condition of the steps and railings. Make sure the rise and run of the steps are consistent to prevent trip hazards. Some common comments:

"UNEVEN STEP RISER HEIGHT IS A TRIP HAZARD. REPAIR."

"SEVERAL LOOSE BRICKS PRESENT ON STEPS. REPAIR."

"EXCESSIVE SETTLING OF MASONRY STEPS. REPAIR."

11. Exterior electrical receptacles. Check to see if there are receptacles at the front and at the back. Also check if they are GFI or not. Mark "GFI" or "NO GFI" next to this item. Some common comments:

"NO OUTLET AT REAR."

"NO OUTLET AT FRONT."

87

"NO EXTERIOR OUTLETS PRESENT."

12. <u>Exterior plumbing fixtures</u>. Check to see if there are faucets at the front and at the back. Some common comments:

"NO FAUCET AT FRONT."

"NO FAUCET AT REAR."

"REAR FAUCET NOT ANCHORED; SECURE TO FOUNDATION."

6.3 ROOFING

This section describes the procedure to use for inspecting the Roofing. The required Roofing inspection sheet can be found in Chapter 5 for you to follow and help guide you through the inspection. Each numbered item listed below corresponds to the numbered item on the inspection sheet.

1. <u>Roofing material condition</u>. Check the general condition of the roof with your binoculars. Make sure you look at all roof surfaces. Write the type of roof (asphalt/fiberglass, wood shakes, slate, metal, etc.) right next to this item. NOTE: Never walk on a wood or slate roof! You could crack it and cause leaks. (You should not be on the roof anyway!) You can sometimes estimate the age of the roof by the age of the house, using the 20 year rule for asphalt/ fiberglass shingles. Some common comments:

"EXCESSIVE BLISTERING OF SHINGLES INDICATES VERY SHORT REMAINING ROOF LIFE."

"EXCESSIVE GRANULE WEAR IN SECTIONS INDICATES SHORT REMAINING ROOF LIFE."

2. Roofing properly installed. Look at the way the roofing material is installed. Look for shingles that are grossly out of alignment, loose, or poorly installed. A common comment:

"UNEVEN SHINGLE ROWS INDICATE POOR WORKMANSHIP."

3. Missing shingles. Check for any missing shingles. A common comment:

"SHINGLES TABS (3 TOTAL) MISSING FROM NORTHEAST SECTION OF ROOF. REPAIR."

4. Shingle blisters/curled edges. This item is usually linked with item number 1. Some common comments:

"SLIGHT BLISTERING OF SHINGLES OBSERVED. NORMAL FOR A ROOF OF THIS AGE. ESTIMATE NEED FOR REPLACEMENT IN 5 YEARS."

5. Roof moss/mildew. Check for any moss growth (green) or any mildew growth (black stains). This is usually found on the north side or under low-hanging tree branches. Some common comments:

"MOSS GROWTH AT NORTH CORNER. RECOMMEND REMOVAL WITH BLEACH/WATER SOLUTION, THEN APPLY ANTI-MOSS METAL STRIP TO UPPER ROW OF SHINGLES."

"SIGNIFICANT MILDEW GROWTH AT NORTH CORNER. RECOMMEND REMOVAL WITH BLEACH/WATER SOLUTION."

6. Flashing adequate. Look for loose, missing, or poorly installed flashing around chimneys, dormers, etc. A common comment:

"LOOSE AND MISSING FLASHING AROUND CHIMNEY. RECOMMEND REPAIR BY QUALIFIED ROOFER."

7. Cracks/gaps in roofing. You must check this one from the attic area. While in the attic area, look for anyplace in the roof where you can see daylight (except for ventilation areas). Some common comments:

"GAP OBSERVED IN ATTIC AREA AROUND MAIN PLUMBING VENT. REPAIR TO PREVENT LEAKAGE."

"GAP OBSERVED IN ATTIC AREA AROUND CHIMNEY. REPAIR TO PREVENT LEAKAGE."

8. Evidence of leaks. You must check this one from the attic area. While in the attic area, look for anyplace on the underside of the subroofing that is significantly stained or discolored from leaks. A common comment:

"WET SUBROOF IN SOUTHWEST CORNER OF ATTIC INDICATES ACTIVE LEAK. REPAIR."

"STAINED SUBROOF IN SOUTHWEST CORNER OF ATTIC INDICATES PAST LEAK. RECOMMEND OBSERVATION OF THIS AREA DURING NEXT RAINFALL TO DETERMINE IF LEAK IS STILL ACTIVE."

9. Skylights watertight. Check the interior area around the skylight for any stains or discolorations caused by water. NOTE: Many stains around skylights are caused by condensation, and not by leaks. A common comment:

"STAINS AROUND INTERIOR NORTH SKYLIGHT INDICATE SLIGHT LEAK OR CONDENSATION PROBLEM."

10. Gutter/downspout condition. Check for any loose, missing, clogged, leaking, or uneven gutters or downspouts. Some common comments:

"MOST GUTTERS CLOGGED WITH LEAVES. RECOMMEND CLEANING."

"MISSING DOWNSPOUT ELBOWS AT NORTH AND WEST CORNERS. REPLACE."

"FRONT GUTTER POORLY SLOPED. REPAIR TO FORM SLOPE TOWARD DOWNSPOUTS."

"SECTION OF GUTTER MISSING FROM REAR OF HOUSE. REPAIR/
REPLACE."

6.4 FOUNDATION

This section describes the procedure to use for inspecting the Foundation. The required Foundation inspection sheet can be found in Chapter 5 for you to follow and help guide you through the inspection. Each numbered item listed below corresponds to the numbered item on the inspection sheet.

1. Foundation material & workmanship. Check the foundation for proper materials and workmanship. If the basement is finished or partly finished where the foundation walls cannot be readily observed, write the following on the first line of the comment section:

"NOTE: FOUNDATION WALLS NOT TOTALLY ACCESSIBLE DUE TO FINISHED BASEMENT."

A common comment:

"UNEVEN MASONRY UNITS INDICATE POOR WORKMANSHIP."

2. Foundation mortar deteriorating. If the foundation uses masonry units (concrete blocks), check the mortar for deterioration. Look for obvious patchwork and try to find out why the patchwork is there. Were there prior settlement problems? Did a car or tractor hit that

area? Was the area damaged during backfilling? If the units are pushed in, this is likely the case. Some common comments:

"MORTAR DETERIORATION ON SOUTH SIDE EXTERIOR DUE TO WATER DAMAGE. RECOMMEND REPAIR."

"PATCHWORK OBSERVED AT SOUTHEAST CORNER. RECOMMEND CHECK WITH CURRENT HOMEOWNER TO DETERMINE REASON FOR PATCH."

3. Settling: Cracks in walls. Look for any visible cracks. Note that most cracks you find will be masonry shrinkage cracks. Occasionally you will find settlement cracks. Pay particular attention to any cracks, as most homebuyers are particularly concerned with these cracks. Some common comments:

"SEVERAL SMALL CRACKS OBSERVED IN SOUTH AND WEST FOUNDATION WALLS DUE TO NORMAL CONCRETE SHRINKAGE. NOT STRUCTURALLY SIGNIFICANT." If it is a newly constructed home, add this: "RECOMMEND MONITOR CRACKS FOR WIDENING OVER THE NEXT 12 MONTHS."

"LARGE CRACKS OBSERVED IN NORTHWEST CORNER. THESE ARE SETTLEMENT CRACKS AND RECOMMEND THIS AREA BE REPAIRED TO PREVENT FUTURE STRUCTURAL PROBLEMS."

4. Settling: Cracks in slab. Look for any cracks in basement or garage slabs. Determine

if they are shrinkage cracks or settlement cracks. Some common comments:

"SEVERAL SHRINKAGE CRACKS OBSERVED NEAR CENTER OF BASEMENT SLAB. NOT STRUCTURALLY SIGNIFICANT."

"SETTLEMENT CRACK OBSERVED IN EAST CORNER OF GARAGE SLAB. RECOMMEND REPAIR."

5. Settling: Slab level. Check if the slab is level. Sometimes a slab will settle without cracking. A common comment:

"GARAGE SLAB IS SIGNIFICANTLY OUT OF LEVEL DUE TO SETTLEMENT. PROBABLE CAUSE IS POOR COMPACTION OF BASE" or "PROBABLE CAUSE IS WATER INFILTRATION OF BASE."

6. Settling: Roof/wall deflections. Look carefully for any deflections in the roof or walls. If you see anything significantly out of level or plumb, you can bet that some type of structural problem is or was present. It could be water damage/rot, termites or carpenter ants, or construction with undersized materials. A common comment:

"SIGNIFICANT WALL DEFLECTION OBSERVED ON EAST SIDE UPPER LEVEL. RECOMMEND TEAR AWAY SMALL SECTION OF WALL TO THOROUGHLY INVESTIGATE."

7. Moisture: Water marks. Look for any evidence of past water infiltration of the foundation walls, and determine if the moisture is from leakage or condensation. If the

basement walls are painted, look for flaking paint. Some common comments:

"MOISTURE OBSERVED AT SOUTH CORNER OF CRAWLSPACE WALL DUE TO POOR EXTERIOR DRAINAGE (SEE "EXTERIOR" SECTION).

"SLIGHT MOISTURE OBSERVED ON CRAWLSPACE WALLS. PROBABLE CAUSE IS CONDENSATION DUE TO POOR VENTILATION AND POOR VAPOR BARRIER."

"EFFLORESCENCE ON INTERIOR CRAWLSPACE WALLS AT WEST CORNER. PROBABLE CAUSE IS POOR EXTERIOR DRAINAGE (SEE "EXTERIOR" SECTION).

"PEELING PAINT ON FOUNDATION WALLS INDICATE EXCESSIVE MOISTURE INFILTRATION OR POOR SURFACE PREPARATION."

8. Moisture: Fungus/mildew growth. Look for fungus or mildew growth on foundation walls. A common comment:

"FUNGUS GROWTH ON CRAWLSPACE WALLS DUE TO EXCESSIVE MOISTURE AND POOR VENTILATION."

9. Moisture: Musty odor. If the basement has a distinct musty odor, report it here. A common comment:

"MUSTY ODOR IN BASEMENT DUE TO POOR VENTILATION."

95

10. Basement floor drain. Any basement should have a floor drain of some type. If a sump pump is present, report it here. Some common comments:

"NO FLOOR DRAIN OBSERVED."

"SUMP PUMP OBSERVED. RECOMMEND CHECK WITH CURRENT HOMEOWNER TO DETERMINE FREQUENCY OF SUMP PUMP OPERATION."

11. Crawlspace ventilation. Look for adequate crawlspace vents. Crawlspaces must be well ventilated. A common comment:

"POOR CRAWLSPACE VENTILATION OBSERVED. RECOMMEND ADD LARGE VENT AT CRAWLSPACE ENTRANCE TO INCREASE VENTILATION."

12. Crawlspace vapor barrier. Check the crawlspace vapor barrier. All sections of the crawlspace should have a barrier. Some common comments:

"NO VAPOR BARRIER PRESENT AT CRAWLSPACE FLOOR. RECOMMEND ADD AT LEAST 6 MIL PLASTIC BARRIER TO ENTIRE CRAWLSPACE FLOOR."

"MISSING SECTIONS OF VAPOR BARRIER AT CRAWLSPACE FLOOR. REPLACE TO COVER ENTIRE FLOOR."

6.5 FRAMING

This section describes the procedure to use for inspecting the Framing. The required Framing inspection sheet can be found in Chapter 5 for you to follow and help guide you through the inspection. Each numbered item listed below corresponds to the numbered item on the inspection sheet.

1. <u>Main beam condition</u>. Check the condition of the main beam. Look for any cracks, splits, or poor support by the foundation or piers. A common comment:

"SPLIT IN MAIN BEAM OBSERVED DUE TO OVERSPAN OF PIERS. RECOMMEND ADD ADDITIONAL PIER DIRECTLY UNDER DAMAGED AREA OF BEAM."

2. <u>Floor joist size/type</u>. Look at the exposed floor joists for adequate size, spacing, and span. In the box beside the item, write the joist size and spacing, i.e. "2x10 16 O.C.". A common comment:

"JOIST SIZE AND SPACING ARE MINIMALLY ACCEPTABLE."

3. <u>Floor joist deflection</u>. Look for any obvious deflections in the floors. Check the structural stability of stairs. Some common comments:

"SIGNIFICANT DEFLECTION OBSERVED IN LIVING ROOM FLOOR FROM OVERSPANNED FLOOR JOISTS. RECOMMEND ADD SISTER JOISTS

TO PROVIDE ADDITIONAL SUPPORT."

"POOR ATTACHMENT OF STAIR STRINGERS OBSERVED IN BASEMENT STAIRS. RECOMMEND REINFORCE ATTACHMENT OF STRINGERS TO FRAMING."

4. Subflooring size/type. From the basement or crawlspace, check the APA markings on the subfloor for thickness. Write the thickness, if found, next to this item, i.e., "23/32"". A common comment:

"EXCESSIVE SUBFLOOR MOVEMENT WHILE WALKING INDICATES UNDERSIZED OR POORLY SUPPORTED SUBFLOOR. RECOMMEND REINFORCEMENT OF SUBFLOOR."

5. Subflooring deflection. Look for obvious deflections on the floors. A common comment:

"SIGNIFICANT DEFLECTION OBSERVED IN LIVING ROOM FLOOR DUE TO OVERSPAN OF FLOOR JOISTS. SEE ITEM 3 ABOVE."

6. Wall stud size/type. Use your stud finder at one or two locations at load bearing walls to determine adequate stud spacing. 2x4 walls should be at least 16" O.C. A common comment:

"MOST WALLS NOT ACCESSIBLE."

7. Wall stud deflection. Look for obvious deflections in walls. This could be due to water,

termites, poor workmanship, or warped studs. A common comment:

"SIGNIFICANT WALL DEFLECTION OBSERVED AT NORTH WALL OF FAMILY ROOM. RECOMMEND TEAR AWAY SECTION OF WALL TO INVESTIGATE FURTHER."

8. Roof rafter/truss size/type. Look at roof rafters or trusses to determine if they are adequate. A common comment:

"MINIMALLY ACCEPTABLE SIZED RAFTERS USED FOR ROOF SUPPORT."

9. Roof rafter/truss deflection. Look for obvious deflections in the roof. This could be due to water, termites, poor workmanship, or warped studs. If a ridge beam is present, check for deflection. Some common comments:

"SIGNIFICANT ROOF DEFLECTION OBSERVED AT NORTHWEST CORNER DUE TO ROTTED TRUSS. RECOMMEND REPAIR IMMEDIATELY TO PREVENT STRUCTURAL INSTABILITY."

"SLIGHT DEFLECTION OBSERVED IN RIDGE BEAM. NOT STRUCTURALLY SIGNIFICANT."

10. Roof sheathing size/type. From the attic area, check the APA (American Plywood Association) markings on the subroof for thickness. Write the thickness, if found, next to this item, i.e., "7/16"". A common comment:

"NO APA MARKINGS ON ROOF SHEATHING."

11. <u>Roof sheathing deflection</u>. Look for obvious deflections on the roof. A common comment:

"SIGNIFICANT DEFLECTION OBSERVED IN VARIOUS ROOF SECTIONS DUE TO DELAMINATION OF SUBROOF.

12. <u>Framing dry and firm</u>. Check the framing for dryness and firmness. This especially applies to crawlspace framing. Wet crawlspaces often contribute to mildew and a high moisture content of wood framing. Use your moisture meter in questionable areas to determine if there is a problem. Some common comments:

"SOME FUNGUS GROWTH OBSERVED ON CRAWLSPACE FRAMING. MOISTURE CONTENT OF FRAMING MEASURED AT 24% INDICATES EXCESSIVE MOISTURE PRESENT. THIS MOISTURE MUST BE BROUGHT DOWN TO ACCEPTABLE LEVEL TO HELP PREVENT SIGNIFICANT DETERIORATION OF FRAMING."

"ROTTED SILL PLATE IN SOUTH CORNER DUE TO MOISTURE FROM THE EXTERIOR. REPAIR."

6.6 INSULATION

This section describes the procedure to use for inspecting the Insulation. The required Insulation inspection sheet can be found in Chapter 5 for you to follow and help guide you through the inspection. Each numbered item listed below corresponds to the numbered item on the inspection sheet.

1. <u>Attic insulation: R =</u>_____ . Measure the thickness of the insulation in the attic with your tape measure and put the estimated R value here. If batts are present, lift one up and observe the stamped R rating. Write down the type of insulation (blown or batts, and fiberglass or rock wool or cellulose) in the space beside the R value. Some common comments:

"R-19 IS MINIMAL FOR THIS AREA. R-30 IS NOW RECOMMENDED FOR THIS AREA."

"BLOWN INSULATION DEPTH IS UNEVEN. REDISTRIBUTE AND FLUFF TO FORM CONSISTENT BLANKET."

"LOOSE AND MISSING BATTS OBSERVED. REPLACE/ADD BATTS TO FORM A CONSISTENT BLANKET."

2. <u>Attic hatch insulation</u>. If the attic is only accessible through a hatch in the ceiling, check for an insulation batt covering the hatch. A common comment:

"MISSING INSULATION BATT OVER ATTIC HATCH. RECOMMEND ADD R-25 BATT."

3. Attic ventilation adequate. Check for adequate attic ventilation. A common comment:

"POOR ATTIC VENTILATION OBSERVED. RECOMMEND ADD VENTS TO INCREASE VENTILATION."

4. Wall insulation: R = _____ . If accessible, write the R value in the blank. The wall insulation will usually be covered with wallboard, paneling, or other material. Look for any open areas (utility rooms, under stairs, etc.) that have any areas where the wall insulation can be seen. Note that any found wall insulation is just a clue, and is not an indication that all walls are equally insulated. If wall insulation is not accessible, write "Not accessible" in the space directly beside this item, and write a dash "-" in the "No Problem" box. A common comment:

"WALL INSULATION NOT TOTALLY ACCESSIBLE DUE TO FINISHED WALLS."

5. Floor/crawlspace insulation: R = _____ . Use the same procedure as in Item 4, above. A common comment:

"MISSING OR LOOSE BATTS OBSERVED IN CRAWLSPACE AREA. REPAIR."

6. Evidence of vapor barrier problems. Look for any signs of vapor barrier problems such

as moist wallboard or mildew on interior wallboard. A common comment:

"MILDEW STAINS OBSERVED ON INTERIOR WALLS INDICATES POSSIBLE VAPOR BARRIER PROBLEM.   RECOMMEND ADDITIONAL PROBING OF WALL TO DETERMINE IF REQUIRED VAPOR BARRIER IS PRESENT."

7. Double/triple pane windows. Check for double or triple pane windows. Circle the word "Double" if double pane or circle the word "triple" if triple pane. If storm windows are present, check the "Minimal" box and write "SINGLE PANE WITH STORMS."

8. Door/window weatherstripping. Check for the presence of weatherstripping and its condition. Look for light entering around the perimeter of doors to indicate poor weatherstripping. Some common comments:

"POOR WEATHERSTRIPPING OBSERVED AROUND FRONT AND SIDE DOORS. REPAIR."

"POOR SEALS AROUND MANY WINDOWS."

6.7 ELECTRICAL

This section describes the procedure to use for inspecting the Electrical system. The required Electrical inspection sheet can be found in Chapter 5 for you to follow and help guide you through the inspection. Each numbered item listed below corresponds to the numbered item on the inspection sheet.

WARNING - WARNING - WARNING - WARNING

In many houses, you may want to carefully remove the main circuit panel cover to expose the wiring. The decision to remove this panel is left up to you, and depends on your personal comfort level and preference with this action. If you decide to remove this cover, you must always use extreme caution when removing this panel!! NEVER remove a panel, or even go near the panel, if any loose or open wiring is present or if you judge the area to be hazardous. Just write down that area is not accessible due to an unsafe condition, and recommend that it be corrected and inspected by a licensed electrician. ALWAYS assume that every wire is energized!

1. Amp service adequate. Check the amp service for the house, as indicated by the size of the wire coming in from the meter. Note that the number listed on the main breaker may not always be what the service amperage is. Write the amp service directly on this line, i.e. "200 amp." The determination of adequate amperage depends on the size of the house. Any house without 220 volt service is considered inadequate, and houses (except very small houses) with less than 60 amps are considered inadequate. Some common comments:

"110 VOLT/60 AMP SERVICE IS CONSIDERED INADEQUATE. RECOMMEND UPGRADE TO 220 VOLT/200 AMP SERVICE."

"220 VOLT/60 AMP SERVICE IS MINIMAL FOR THIS SIZE OF HOUSE. EXPECT PROBLEMS IF NUMEROUS ELECTRIC APPLIANCES WILL BE USED."

2. <u>Adequate number of circuits</u>.   Observe the number of fuses or breakers present, and determine if there are enough circuits for the size of the house. Some common comments:

"ONLY SIX CIRCUITS OBSERVED. THIS IS A LOW NUMBER FOR THE SIZE OF THIS HOUSE AND ITS ELECTRICAL SERVICE.   RECOMMEND COMPLETE DETAILED INSPECTION BY QUALIFIED ELECTRICIAN."

3. <u>Main circuit panel condition</u>. Check the overall condition of the main panel. Some common comments:

"NO SECURING COLLARS ON TWO WIRES ENTERING PANEL. REPAIR."

"PANEL DOOR MISSING. REPAIR OR REPLACE."

"PANEL POORLY SECURED TO WALL. RECOMMEND REPAIR BY QUALIFIED ELECTRICIAN."

4. <u>Circuits labeled</u>.   Check for labels. NOTE: Many times the circuits are incorrectly labeled! A common comment:

"ONLY PARTIAL LABELING OBSERVED."

5. <u>Fuses/breakers adequate</u>.   Check the general condition of the fuses or breakers, and look for any open areas or missing cover plates in the main panel. Look for signs of overloading in the main panel, usually indicated by dark spots or burns near the fuses or

105

breakers. Check the condition and size of the wires coming into the main panel. The only way to thoroughly check for proper wire size is to remove the main panel cover (see WARNING at the beginning of this section). If you prefer to remove this cover, check that the proper sized wire is feeding a properly sized breaker or fuse. For example, a 14 gauge wire (or larger) can have a 15 amp breaker, but cannot feed a 20 amp (or higher) breaker. A 12 gauge wire (or larger) can have a 20 amp breaker, but cannot feed a 30 amp (or higher) breaker, etc. Also, check for aluminum wiring, and indicate its presence. Some common comments:

"OPEN SPACE AT ONE BREAKER LOCATION. RECOMMEND QUALIFIED ELECTRICIAN COVER THIS SPACE IMMEDIATELY TO REDUCE SHOCK HAZARD."

"PENNY OBSERVED IN PLACE OF FUSE. DANGER! RECOMMEND IMMEDIATE REMOVAL OF PENNY BY QUALIFIED ELECTRICIAN AND CHECKOUT OF POSSIBLE PROBLEMS IN THAT CIRCUIT."

"BURN MARKS NEAR HOT WATER HEATER BREAKER INDICATES PAST PROBLEM. RECOMMEND INVESTIGATE WITH CURRENT HOMEOWNER OR QUALIFIED ELECTRICIAN."

"UNDERSIZED WIRES AND/OR OVERSIZED FUSES OBSERVED INSIDE MAIN PANEL. DANGER! RECOMMEND IMMEDIATE INSPECTION AND CORRECTION BY QUALIFIED ELECTRICIAN."

"POSSIBLE ALUMINUM WIRING OBSERVED IN MAIN PANEL.

RECOMMEND CHECK OF PROPER INSTALLATION BY QUALIFIED ALUMINUM WIRING ELECTRICIAN."

6. 20+ amp circuit for kitchen. Check the amperage for circuits going to the kitchen. Due to its many electrical appliances, the kitchen should have at least a 20 amp circuit. A common comment:

"ONLY 15 AMP CIRCUIT TO KITCHEN. RECOMMEND AT LEAST 20 AMP."

7. 20+ amp circuit for laundry. Same as item 6, above.

8. 30+ amp circuit for heat/AC. Same as item 6, above.

9. 30+ amp circuit for hot water. Same as item 6, above.

10. Exterior service condition. Check the general condition of the exterior service. Some common comments:

"WORN INSULATION ON MAIN FEED WIRE AT GROUND LEVEL. DANGER! RECOMMEND REPAIR BY UTILITY COMPANY OR QUALIFIED ELECTRICIAN."

"METER DAMAGE OBSERVED. RECOMMEND REPAIR BY UTILITY COMPANY OR QUALIFIED ELECTRICIAN."

11. <u>Receptacle condition</u>. Check for any uncovered receptacles, uncovered junction boxes, missing junction boxes, exposed wiring, and damaged or loose receptacles. Check the general spacing of receptacles. Some common comments:

"OPEN WIRE CONNECTION OBSERVED IN ATTIC AREA NEAR ACCESS HATCH. MUST ENCLOSE IN JUNCTION BOX."

"NUMEROUS RECEPTACLES LOOSE AND REQUIRE SECURING."

"COVERS MISSING FROM THREE JUNCTION BOXES IN BASEMENT AREA. REPAIR."

"ONLY ONE OR TWO RECEPTACLES PER ROOM MAY CAUSE INCONVENIENCE OR OVERLOADING."

12. <u>Receptacles properly grounded</u>. Check receptacles using the circuit tester, and note any wiring errors. Some common comments:

"LOOSE OR MISSING GROUND AT TWO RECEPTACLES IN NORTHWEST BEDROOM AT SOUTH WALL. REPAIR."

"HOT/NEUTRAL WIRES REVERSED AT ALL GARAGE RECEPTACLES. REPAIR."

6.8 PLUMBING

This section describes the procedure to use for inspecting the Plumbing system. The required Plumbing inspection sheet can be found in Chapter 5 for you to follow and help guide you through the inspection. Each numbered item listed below corresponds to the numbered item on the inspection sheet.

1. <u>Water supply pressure/flow rate</u>. Check the water supply pressure and flow rate by turning on the bathroom and kitchen hot and cold faucets and visually observing the flow. Flush a toilet and run the faucets and observe any significant drop in water pressure. Report minimal or low pressures as minor or possibly major items, depending on the severity of the problem. Some common comments:

"MINIMAL SUPPLY PRESSURE OBSERVED."

"LOW HOT WATER FLOW RATE IN MASTER BATHROOM SHOWER. RECOMMEND PLUMBER CHECK FOR BLOCKAGE."

2. <u>Water supply piping size/material</u>. Observe the visible supply pipe size and material. These are usually in the basement or crawlspace. Also check to see if these pipes are adequately supported. Some common comments:

"PIPES POORLY SUPPORTED IN CRAWLSPACE. RECOMMEND ADD PROPER SUPPORTS EVERY 48 INCHES."

"OLDER GALVANIZED STEEL PIPES ARE SUBJECT TO BLOCKAGE OVER TIME."

"POSSIBLE LEAD PIPE AT SERVICE ENTRANCE. RECOMMEND FURTHER INVESTIGATION AND REPLACEMENT OF ANY LEAD PIPES IN SYSTEM."

"INADEQUATELY SIZED MAIN SUPPLY LINE (1/2" COPPER) RESULTS IN MARGINAL FLOW RATES. RECOMMEND USING AT LEAST 3/4" COPPER FOR MAIN LINE."

3. Water supply shut off valve. Locate the main water supply shut off valve, and always point out its location to your client. Explain that if there is a leak anywhere in the house, just turn this valve to shut off all water until the leak can be fixed. If the valve cannot be located, write "NOT FOUND" in the space beside the item. A common comment:

"VALVE NOT FOUND. RECOMMEND ASK CURRENT HOMEOWNER FOR LOCATION."

4. Dielectric couplings. Check if any dissimilar metals are joined at any couplings or pipe supports (i.e., galvanized connected to copper). This type of coupling is incorrect and will result in severe corrosion due to galvanic chemical reactions. Some common comments:

"STEEL STRAPS SUPPORTING COPPER PIPES IN CRAWLSPACE, RESULTING IN CORROSION OF STRAPS. RECOMMEND REPLACE STEEL WITH COPPER OR NON-CONDUCTIVE SUPPORTS."

110

"STEEL/COPPER CONNECTION NEAR CRAWLSPACE ENTRANCE WILL RESULT IN INTERNAL CORROSION OF STEEL PIPE. RECOMMEND INSTALL PROPER NON-CONDUCTIVE COUPLING."

5. <u>Water hammer problem</u>. Check for water hammer problems by turning on all internal faucets to fully open and quickly closing them. If a loud knocking sound is heard, it is either a water hammer problem or a poorly supported supply pipe. A common comment:

"LOUD KNOCK OBSERVED AT KITCHEN FAUCET. PROBABLE CAUSES ARE FAUCET ASSEMBLY OR POORLY SUPPORTED SUPPLY LINE. RECOMMEND PLUMBER INVESTIGATE AND REPAIR."

6. <u>Evidence of supply leaks</u>. Look under sinks, on walls, in crawlspaces, and especially on first floor ceilings below bathrooms for any signs of present or past water leaks. Some common comments:

"ACTIVE WATER SUPPLY LEAK OBSERVED IN CRAWLSPACE. REPAIR IMMEDIATELY."

"WATER STAINS ON LIVING ROOM CEILING INDICATE PAST WATER LEAKAGE. RECOMMEND ASK HOMEOWNER ABOUT HISTORY OF LEAK."

7. <u>Kitchen/bath sink shut off valves</u>. Check each sink for the presence of shut off valves for the hot and cold water supplies. A common comment:

"NO SHUT OFF VALVES PRESENT IN LOWER LEVEL BATHROOM

111

SINK."

8. <u>Drain piping size/material</u>. Observe the physical size and the material used for the primary and secondary drain lines. These are usually visible in the basement or crawlspace areas. A common comment:

"INADEQUATELY SIZED DRAIN LINE OBSERVED AT BASEMENT CEILING FOR FIRST LEVEL TOILET. LINE SHOULD NOT BE SMALLER THAN 3-1/2 TO 4 INCH DIAMETER. REPAIR/REPLACE."

9. <u>Drainage rate adequate</u>. Run water in the sinks and tubs and observe the adequacy of drainage. Report if any drains are slow. A common comment:

"SLOW DRAIN OBSERVED AT KITCHEN SINK. REPAIR."

10. <u>Drain traps in place</u>. Check for the presence of P-traps at each sink or fixture. Report any lack of a P-trap or the presence of an older S-trap. (S-traps tend to create suction that pulls water out of the trap and allows sewer gas to escape into the room.) Some common comments:

"OLDER S-TRAP OBSERVED AT KITCHEN SINK. RECOMMEND REPLACE WITH P-TRAP."

"NO TRAP PRESENT IN LOWER LEVEL BATHROOM SINK. RECOMMEND IMMEDIATE INSTALLATION OF TRAP TO PREVENT SEWER GASES FROM ENTERING HOUSE."

11. <u>Drain venting adequate</u>. Look outside on the roof for drain vent pipes. Also, turn on faucets on and listen for gurgling noises after the sink bowl has drained. Excessive gurgling usually indicates that the venting for that fixture is inadequate. A common comment:

"GURGLING SOUND AT KITCHEN SINK INDICATES POOR DRAIN VENTING. RECOMMEND FURTHER INSPECTION BY QUALIFIED PLUMBER."

12. <u>Evidence of sewer backup problem</u>. Look for signs of past or present sewage backups, including damp, smelly areas in basements or crawlspaces. For homes with septic systems, look for damp areas in the drain field that would indicate a blocked drain line. For any septic system, always refer your client to a septic specialist, because the ONLY way to properly inspect a septic system is to pump it out and visually inspect the tank and visible lines. The septic contractor may also run water in the house for a certain period of time to check the drainage rate of the field. Some common comments:

"NO VISIBLE SIGNS OF SEPTIC SYSTEM PROBLEMS, BUT RECOMMEND THOROUGH CLEAN-OUT AND INSPECTION BY QUALIFIED SEPTIC SPECIALIST."

"DAMP GROUND AREA IN SEPTIC FIELD INDICATES POSSIBLE SEPTIC SYSTEM BLOCKAGE. RECOMMEND THOROUGH INSPECTION BY QUALIFIED SEPTIC SPECIALIST."

13. <u>Hot water heater capacity</u>. Observe the name plate on water heater and read the capacity in gallons. Write this capacity on the line next to this item, i.e., "52 GAL." Report as a problem if the tank capacity is too small for the size of the house. A common comment:

113

"40 GALLON ELECTRIC TANK IS MINIMAL FOR TYPICAL 2-1/2 BATH HOUSE."

14. Hot water heater condition. Observe the general condition of the tank, and make sure a pressure-temperature relief valve is installed. Look at the nameplate for the serial number to determine the year of manufacture; write the age in years next to this item, i.e., "9 YEARS OLD." Most importantly, look at the bottom of the tank for rust; this rust indicates that the inner liner leaks and the tank needs replaced soon. Some common comments:

"DANGER! NO PRESSURE-TEMPERATURE RELIEF VALVE INSTALLED. RECOMMEND IMMEDIATE INSTALLATION OF VALVE BY QUALIFIED PLUMBER."

"RUST AT BOTTOM OF TANK INDICATES VERY SHORT REMAINING LIFE. RECOMMEND REPLACE."

"OLDER MODEL IS RELATIVELY INEFFICIENT AND NEAR END OF SERVICE LIFE. RECOMMEND REPLACE."

6.9 HEATING / COOLING

This section describes the procedure to use for inspecting the Heating/Cooling system. The required Heating/Cooling inspection sheet can be found in Chapter 5 for you to follow and help guide you through the inspection. Each numbered item listed below corresponds to the numbered item on the inspection sheet.

1. <u>System Type:</u>   Observe the type of system and write it on the line next to this item, i.e., "HEAT PUMP" or "GAS FURNACE + AC" or "OIL FURNACE + AC" or similar. Visually observe the size of the unit to determine if it is undersized or oversized. A common comment:

"UNIT APPEARS UNDERSIZED FOR THIS SIZE OF HOUSE. RECOMMEND COMPLETE INSPECTION BY SPECIALIZED HVAC CONTRACTOR."

2. <u>Estimate of heating/cooling efficiency.</u>   With the thermostat off, measure the air temperature at a vent or register. Turn on the system and observe the temperature approximately 10 minutes later to determine heating or cooling efficiency. [NOTE: Do not test AC if outside temperature is below 65 deg F; you could possibly damage the unit (depends on the manufacturer).]   Some common comments:

"A/C NOT TESTED DUE TO LOW OUTSIDE AIR TEMPERATURE OF 55ºF."

"POOR HEAT OUTPUT OBSERVED AT REGISTERS BY TEMPERATURE TEST. RECOMMEND THOROUGH SYSTEM CHECK BY QUALIFIED HVAC TECHNICIAN."

"POOR A/C OUTPUT OBSERVED AT REGISTERS BY TEMPERATURE TEST. RECOMMEND THOROUGH SYSTEM CHECK BY QUALIFIED HVAC TECHNICIAN."

3. Compressor unit condition. For homes with heat pumps or A/C, visually inspect the condition of the exterior compressor unit. Look for bent fins, physical damage, oil leakage at the compressor, excessive rust around the compressor, and the general age and condition of the unit. With the system on, check for proper fan rotation and listen for any strange noises. Some common comments:

"NUMEROUS BENT FINS ON EXTERIOR UNIT. RECOMMEND STRAIGHTEN FINS WITH FIN COMB TO INCREASE EFFICIENCY."

"EXTERIOR A/C UNIT IS OLDER, RELATIVELY INEFFICIENT MODEL. RECOMMEND CHECK WITH CURRENT HOMEOWNER AS TO PREVIOUS REPAIRS TO DETERMINE COMPRESSOR AGE."

"EXTERIOR FAN NOT OPERATIONAL. REPAIR."

4. Compressed freon line insulated. Visually inspect the freon line for insulation. Report any old or missing insulation. A common comment:

"MISSING OR CRACKED SECTIONS OF FREON LINE INSULATION. REPLACE INSULATION."

5. Compressor unit level & ventilated. Check the outside unit for level and proper ventilation area. Some common comments:

"OUTSIDE UNIT NOT LEVEL. REPAIR."

"OUTSIDE UNIT TOO CLOSE TO HOUSE FOR EFFICIENT VENTILATION. RECOMMEND MOVE UNIT AT LEAST TWO FEET FROM HOUSE."

"OUTSIDE UNIT VENTILATION PARTIALLY BLOCKED BY VEGETATION. REMOVE VEGETATION TO INCREASE VENTILATION."

6. Interior unit/furnace condition. Check the condition of the interior unit(s). Observe the age (from the serial number, if possible) and general condition of the unit. For gas or oil furnaces, remove the cover and visually check the flame for proper burning and for excessive dirt and soot buildup. For heat pumps or A/C units, remove any easily removable covers and check the heat exchanger fins for any dirt buildup. For forced air systems, listen for any unusual sounds from the blower. Some common comments:

"SIGNIFICANT ASH/SOOT/DIRT BUILDUP AT GAS BURNERS. RECOMMEND COMPLETE CLEANING AND CHECKUP BY QUALIFIED TECHNICIAN."

"SIGNIFICANT DIRT BUILDUP OBSERVED ON HEAT EXCHANGER FINS. RECOMMEND THOROUGH CLEANING TO INCREASE EFFICIENCY."

"SQUEAKING AFTER BLOWER SHUTDOWN INDICATES FAILING FAN BEARINGS OR NEED FOR LUBRICATION. RECOMMEND COMPLETE CHECKOUT BY QUALIFIED TECHNICIAN."

"GAS FURNACE IS OLDER, RELATIVELY INEFFICIENT MODEL."

117

7. <u>Combustion air availability</u>. For fuel burning systems, check for adequate combustion air by observing the surrounding room size and ventilation openings.

"INADEQUATE VENTILATION OPENINGS IN FURNACE AREA FOR PROPER COMBUSTION. RECOMMEND INCREASING VENTILATION BY ADDITION OF VENT OPENINGS TO DOOR."

8. <u>Condensate drain present</u>. On A/C units, check for the condensate drain line. Make sure a U-trap is present, and the line properly drains to the exterior of the house. Some common comments:

"CONDENSATE DRAINS INTO CRAWLSPACE. MUST EXTEND LINE TO DRAIN TO EXTERIOR."

"WATER AROUND INTERIOR UNIT INDICATES POSSIBLE CONDENSATE LINE BLOCKAGE. RECOMMEND INVESTIGATE AND REPAIR IF NECESSARY."

9. <u>Air filter maintenance</u>. Check for a clean air filter(s) in forced air systems. A comment:

"FILTER DIRTY. REPLACE."

10. <u>Ductwork size/material</u>. Check the airflows on forced air systems. Look at duct sizes and ductwork arrangements if airflow is too low or too high. Observe the number and placement of vents or registers in rooms. Also look for properly sized air returns for forced air systems. Some common comments:

"HIGH AIRFLOW AT SOME VENTS AND LOW AIRFLOW AT OTHER VENTS INDICATES EITHER THE NEED FOR BALANCING WITH A DAMPER OR POORLY DESIGNED DUCTWORK. RECOMMEND THOROUGH SYSTEM CHECK BY QUALIFIED HVAC TECHNICIAN."

"NO REGISTERS PRESENT IN NORTHWEST BEDROOM."

"ONLY ONE REGISTER PRESENT IN LARGE LIVING ROOM AREA. RESULT MAY BE POOR HEATING/COOLING/VENTILATION IN THIS AREA."

"NO AIR RETURN GRILLE AT UPPER LEVEL. MAY RESULT IN POOR VENTILATION OF UPPER LEVEL."

11. <u>Thermostat condition</u>. Observe the operation and general physical condition of the thermostat. A common comment:

"THERMOSTAT HOUSING CRACKED AND LOOSE. RECOMMEND REPLACE."

12. <u>Gas/oil service line</u>. Check the gas (natural or propane) or fuel oil supply lines for adequate material, size, condition, and supports. For oil burners, check the condition of the outside oil storage tank; report any signs of leakage. IMPORTANT: Perform a visual check for any signs of a buried oil tank (ground vents, buried fuel lines, oil leaks at ground); always report this possible environmental hazard with a potential huge price tag to your client. Some common comments:

"POSSIBLE UNDERGROUND OIL TANK AT NORTH SIDE. POSSIBLE ENVIRONMENTAL HAZARD WITH LARGE CLEANUP COST IF TANK HAS LEAKS."

"NATURAL GAS SUPPLY LINE POORLY SUPPORTED IN CRAWLSPACE AREA. RECOMMEND ADD ADDITIONAL SUPPORTS."

6.10 BATHROOMS

This section describes the procedure to use for inspecting the Bathrooms. The required Bathroom inspection sheet can be found in Chapter 5 for you to follow and help guide you through the inspection. Each bathroom must use a separate sheet. Each numbered item listed below corresponds to the numbered item on the inspection sheet.

1. <u>Bathroom layout</u>. Look at the general layout of the bathroom, and report any non-standard conditions such as cramped spaces or low headroom. A common comment:

"INADEQUATE CLEARANCE BETWEEN TOILET EDGE AND SINK."

2. <u>Bathroom sink condition</u>. Look at the general condition of the sink and its fixtures. Run the hot and cold water to check for supply pressure, flow, and for any strange noises. Some common comments:

"SINK IS OLD BUT FUNCTIONAL."

"FIXTURES LOOSE. REPAIR OR REPLACE."

"FAUCET DRIPS. REPAIR OR REPLACE."

"POOR HOT WATER FLOW AT SINK. RECOMMEND CHECK FOR POSSIBLE BLOCKAGE IN SUPPLY LINE."

3. <u>Evidence of water leakage</u>. Look for any present or past signs of water leakage at the sink, tub, and toilet. Some common comments:

"SLIGHT LEAK OBSERVED AT SINK DRAIN TRAP. REPAIR."

"WATER STAINS BELOW SINK DRAIN TRAP INDICATES PAST LEAKAGE. NO PRESENT LEAKS OBSERVED."

4. <u>Bathtub/shower condition</u>. Look at the general condition of the tub or shower and its fixtures. Run the hot and cold water to check for supply pressure, flow, and for any strange noises. Some common comments:

"TUB IS OLD AND STAINED."

"FIXTURES LOOSE. REPAIR OR REPLACE."

"FAUCET DRIPS. REPAIR OR REPLACE."

"POOR HOT WATER FLOW AT SHOWER. RECOMMEND CHECK FOR

121

POSSIBLE BLOCKAGE IN SUPPLY LINE."

"SHOWER HEAD IS EXCESSIVELY LOOSE. REPAIR."

5. <u>Water-resistant surfaces</u>. Check for areas that are incompatible with constant moisture or not sealed against possible water infiltration. Some common comments:

"CAULK AROUND SINK EDGE TO PREVENT WATER INFILTRATION."

"CAULK AROUND UPPER TUB EDGE TO PREVENT WATER INFILTRATION."

"CAULK AT TUB/FLOOR JOINT TO PREVENT WATER INFILTRATION."

6. <u>Toilet condition</u>. Observe the general condition of the toilet. Check the lower bowl and upper tank for stains and cracks. Remove the tank cover, flush, and observe the flapper and fill valve operation. Some common comments:

"WATER RUNS AFTER TANK IS FULL DUE TO WARPED FLAPPER VALVE OR FAULTY FILL VALVE. REPAIR."

"SIGNIFICANT BUILDUP OF MINERAL DEPOSITS INSIDE TANK."

"INNER BOWL STAINED AND DISCOLORED."

"TOILET LOOSE AND WOBBLY. SECURE TO FLOOR."

"TOILET CRACKED AT FLOOR BOLTS DUE TO POSSIBLE OVERTIGHTENING."

7. <u>Bathroom ventilation</u>. Check the condition of the exhaust fan (if present). Make sure either an operable window or fan is present. If only an operable window is present, write "WINDOW ONLY" on the line next to this item. Some common comments:

"EXHAUST FAN VERY NOISY. REPAIR"

"EXHAUST FAN INOPERABLE. REPAIR."

8. <u>Bathroom electrical receptacles</u>. Check if there is at least one electrical receptacle present. Test it with the circuit tester. If it is a GFI receptacle, write "GFI" on the line next to this item. If not a GFI receptacle, write "NON-GFI". A common comment:

"NO RECEPTACLES PRESENT."

9. <u>Bathroom lighting</u>. Check for the adequacy of lighting. A common comment:

"MINIMAL LIGHTING IN THIS AREA."

10. <u>Sufficient heating</u>. Check for the presence of a heating register. A common comment:

"NO HEATING REGISTER PRESENT."

6.11 KITCHEN

This section describes the procedure to use for inspecting the Kitchen. The required Kitchen inspection sheet can be found in Chapter 5 for you to follow and help guide you through the inspection. Each numbered item listed below corresponds to the numbered item on the inspection sheet.

1. Kitchen layout. Check the general layout of the kitchen, and observe the "work triangle" and distance between the stove, sink, and refrigerator. A common comment:

"GENERALLY POOR LAYOUT OF KITCHEN APPLIANCES DUE TO LARGE DISTANCE BETWEEN SINK AND STOVE."

2. Cabinet condition. Check the condition of the cabinet faces, doors, and drawers. Some common comments:

"TWO DRAWERS BROKEN. REPAIR/ADJUST."

"CABINET DOORS NOT LEVEL OR EVEN. ADJUST."

3. Countertop condition. Observe the general condition of the countertops. Look for wear, large nicks, stains, etc. Some common comments:

"COUNTERTOPS ARE OLD AND IN GENERALLY POOR CONDITION."

"LARGE CHIPS OBSERVED IN SEVERAL LOCATIONS ON COUNTERTOPS."

4. <u>Kitchen sink condition</u>.   Observe the overall condition of the sink and faucets. Some general comments:

"CAULK AROUND SINK RIM TO PREVENT WATER INFILTRATION."

"SINK FIXTURES ARE OLD AND WORN. RECOMMEND REPLACE."

"CHIPS AND STAINS OBSERVED IN SINK."

5. <u>Evidence of water leakage</u>. With the water running, look for active water supply or drain leaks under the sink. Also observe the area below the sink for any old water stains that would indicate a prior significant leak. Some common comments:

"SLIGHT LEAK OBSERVED AT SINK DRAIN. REPAIR."

"MODERATE LEAK OBSERVED AT HOT WATER SUPPLY CONNECTION UNDER SINK. REPAIR IMMEDIATELY."

"ROTTED SECTION OF CABINET UNDER SINK INDICATES PAST PROLONGED LEAK. RECOMMEND REPLACE ALL ROTTED AREAS."

6. <u>Garbage disposal condition</u>. Turn on the water, then turn on the garbage disposal (if equipped). Listen for any unnatural sounds. Some common comments:

"DISPOSAL JAMMED; RECOMMEND CHECK FOR OBSTRUCTION BY QUALIFIED PLUMBER."

"DISPOSAL EXCESSIVELY NOISY; INDICATES NEED FOR REPLACEMENT."

"NOTE: A GARBAGE DISPOSAL SHOULD NOT BE USED WITH A SEPTIC SYSTEM."

7. Stove/range condition. Check the overall condition of the stove/range. Check the operation of all burners, and look for any missing or broken pieces. Some common comments:

"RIGHT REAR BURNER INOPERABLE."

"RANGE IS OLDER MODEL AND IN GENERALLY POOR CONDITION."

"LARGE DENT OBSERVED IN FRONT PANEL."

8. Range hood/vent. Observe the condition of the hood/vent. Turn on exhaust fan, check high and low speeds, check the operation of the light (if equipped), and report any discrepancies. Some common comments:

"VENT FAN INOPERABLE. REPAIR."

"VENT FILTER CLOGGED WITH DIRT/GREASE."

"VENT FAN EXCESSIVELY NOISY. REPAIR."

9. Refrigerator condition. Observe the general condition of the refrigerator, inside and out. Open the freezer compartment and check for frozen items. Open the refrigerator section and feel the temperature of any liquid. Be sure to check the setting of the thermostat for these areas. Close the doors and check the gasket for seal integrity around the perimeter of the doors. Some common comments:

"UNIT IS OLDER MODEL WITH LIMITED REMAINING LIFE."

"POOR SEAL AT FREEZER DOOR GASKET. REPAIR."

"UNIT INTERIOR DIRTY AND STAINED."

"MUSTY ODOR OBSERVED AT UNIT INTERIOR. NEEDS CLEANED."

10. Dishwasher condition. Observe the general condition of the dishwasher. Check knobs, door closure, etc. Run the dishwasher until the wash cycle activates; quickly open the door to observe water washing action. Reset the dishwasher to drain; watch and listen at the sink for proper drainage. Some common comments:

"UNIT IS OLDER MODEL WITH LIMITED REMAINING LIFE."

"UNIT INTERIOR DIRTY AND STAINED."

11. Kitchen lighting. Observe the general lighting of the kitchen area. Some common

comments:

"MARGINAL LIGHTING UNDER CABINET AREAS."

"MARGINAL LIGHTING NEAR KITCHEN SINK AREA."

12. Electrical receptacles. Check for locations of electrical receptacles at the countertops, and ensure that they are GFI protected if near the sink. A common comment:

"NO GFI RECEPTACLES PRESENT NEAR SINK."

6.12 INTERIOR

This section describes the procedure to use for inspecting the Interior. The required Interior inspection sheet can be found in Chapter 5 for you to follow and help guide you through the inspection. Each numbered item listed below corresponds to the numbered item on the inspection sheet.

1. Wall condition. Observe the condition of the walls throughout the house, in general terms only. Don't spend a lot of time nit-picking every drywall crack or nailpop; just describe the general condition. However, do report on any large or significant conditions, such as a large hole in the wall or an extensive drywall crack. Some common comments:

"MINOR COSMETIC DRYWALL CRACKS AND NAIL POPS OBSERVED

THROUGHOUT. NOT STRUCTURALLY SIGNIFICANT."

"LARGE HOLE IN DRYWALL IN KITCHEN AREA; REPAIR."

"NUMEROUS PLASTER CRACKS OBSERVED IN UPPER LEVEL; NOT STRUCTURALLY SIGNIFICANT."

"NORMAL WEAR AND TEAR OBSERVED; NEEDS REPAINTED."

2. Ceiling condition. This item inspected and reported in the same manner as the walls (see above), and is usually reported with the same comments as item 1. A common comment:

"DRYWALL CRACK OBSERVED AT UPPER LEVEL CEILING DUE TO TRUSS UPLIFT. NOT STRUCTURALLY SIGNIFICANT."

3. Flooring/carpeting condition. Observe the condition of the floors/carpet throughout the house, in general terms only. Don't spend a lot of time nit-picking; just describe the general condition. However, do report on any large or significant conditions, such as a large hole or stains in the carpet or flooring. Some common comments:

"MINOR CARPET STAINS OBSERVED THROUGHOUT."

"SEVERAL BURNS OBSERVED IN FAMILY ROOM CARPET."

"STAINS AND CRACKS OBSERVED ON KITCHEN FLOORING."

"NORMAL WEAR AND TEAR OBSERVED ON CARPETING THROUGHOUT."

4. <u>Molding & trim</u>. Observe the condition of the molding and trimwork throughout the house, in general terms only. Don't spend a lot of time nit-picking; just describe the general condition. However, do report on any significant conditions, such as poor workmanship or incomplete trimwork. A common comment:

"POOR WORKMANSHIP ON MOLDING IN FAMILY ROOM."

5. <u>Interior doors</u>. Observe the general condition of the interior doors. Open and close each door to see if is properly aligned and if it latches correctly. Some common comments:

"THESE DOORS DO NOT LATCH PROPERLY AND REQUIRE REPAIR OR ADJUSTMENT: NORTHEAST BEDROOM, SOUTH BEDROOM CLOSET, UPPER HALL CLOSET."

"MISSING DOORKNOBS AT LOWER LEVEL UTILITY ROOM DOOR."

6. <u>Condition of windows</u>. Observe the general condition of the windows, from the inside of the house. Open and close one or two windows to determine the ease of opening and closing. Some common comments:

"BROKEN SEAL OBSERVED IN SOUTH BEDROOM DUAL-PANE WINDOW; REPLACE SEALED GLASS UNIT."

"WINDOWS DIFFICULT TO OPEN DUE TO PAINT LAYERS AND AGE OF WINDOWS."

7. Presence of odors. Report any unusual odors that you may observe. A possibe comment:

"STRONG ODOR OF PET URINE IN NORTHWEST BEDROOM."

8. Attic access. Observe the general condition and location of the access hatch or entryway into the attic area. Some common comments:

"POOR ACCESS TO ATTIC DUE TO UNDERSIZED CEILING HATCH."

"POOR ACCESS TO ATTIC DUE TO BLOCKAGE OF HATCH IN CLOSET."

9. Lighting. Observe the general lighting conditions throughout. Some common comments:

"NO OVERHEAD LIGHTS IN BEDROOMS."

"MINIMAL LIGHTING IN UPPER LEVEL HALL."

10. Closet space. Observe, in general, the amount of closet space in the hallways and bedrooms of the house. A common comment:

"MINIMAL CLOSET SPACE THROUGHOUT."

6.13 SAFETY CHECK

This section describes the procedure to use for inspecting the Safety features. The required Safety inspection sheet can be found in Chapter 5 for you to follow and help guide you through the inspection. Each numbered item listed below corresponds to the numbered item on the inspection sheet.

IMPORTANT - IMPORTANT - IMPORTANT!!!! From a personal liability standpoint, consider this section as the most important section of the report. Since this section deals with safety items, always be extra thorough!

1. <u>Bedroom fire escapes</u>. Check each bedroom for an appropriately sized window to the exterior for escape purposes. Window size is determined by building codes. Some common comments:

"ALL BEDROOMS AT UPPER LEVEL; NO ESCAPE LADDERS."

"INADEQUATELY SIZED WINDOW IN LOWER LEVEL BEDROOM; THIS ROOM CANNOT BE USED AS A BEDROOM UNLESS WINDOW IS ENLARGED."

"ENSURE ALL BEDROOM WINDOWS CAN BE EASILY OPENED."

2. <u>Smoke detectors installed</u>. At least one working smoke detector should be installed at every level in the house. If convenient, press the test button to test the alarm. Some common comments:

"NO SMOKE DETECTOR AT LOWER LEVEL. RECOMMEND INSTALL."

"UPPER LEVEL DETECTOR IS OLDER MODEL. RECOMMEND REPLACE."

3. <u>Exterior door deadbolts</u>. Observe the presence of deadbolts or braces for the exterior doors. Some common comments:

"NO DEADBOLTS PRESENT. RECOMMEND INSTALL."

"NO SECURITY BAR AT REAR SLIDING GLASS DOOR. RECOMMEND INSTALL."

4. <u>Window latches/locks</u>. Check the windows for latches or locking mechanisms. A common comment:

"SEVERAL BROKEN OR MISALIGNED LATCHES OBSERVED. REPAIR."

5. <u>GFI circuit in bathrooms</u>. Using the plug-in circuit tester, test the outlet(s) near the sink and/or tub/shower for GFI. Outlets that must or should be protected with GFI are listed in building codes. Some common comments:

"NO GFI PROTECTION IN BATHROOMS. RECOMMEND INSTALL."

"GFI IN MASTER BATH INOPERABLE. REPAIR."

133

6. GFI circuit in kitchen. Same as for item 5.

7. GFI circuit for exterior. Same as for item 5.

8. Exterior stair railings. Check for the presence and/or condition of exterior stair railings, as determined by local building codes. Some common comments:

"LOOSE RAILING AT FRONT PORCH. REPAIR."

"LOOSE RAILING AT REAR DECK. REPAIR."

"NO RAILING PRESENT AT FRONT PORCH STEPS. RECOMMEND ADDING RAILING."

9. Interior stair railings. Check for the presence and/or condition of interior stair railings, as determined by local building codes. Some common comments:

"LOOSE RAILING AT STAIRWAY. REPAIR."

"NO RAILING PRESENT AT STAIRWAY. RECOMMEND ADDING RAILING."

10. Hot water heater venting. This item only applies to gas (or oil) burning hot water systems. Carefully inspect the vent system for leaks, dents, improper bends, and especially too long of a run through too small of a vent pipe. If in doubt about the draw of the vent system, turn the heater on (at the thermostat), let it run for a few minutes, then light a match,

blow the match out, and place the smoking match near the top of the tank vent. Observe if the smoke is sucked in (good draw) or blown back into the room (reverse draw - Bad!), or slightly sucked in (marginal draw - needs work). Ideally, this test should be performed with all doors and windows shut, and all bath and kitchen vent fans on to simulate worst case conditions. Some common comments:

"POOR DRAW OBSERVED AT HOT WATER HEATER VENT. PROBABLE CAUSE IS LONG RUN OF UNDERSIZED 3" DIAMETER VENT PIPE. RECOMMEND INSTALL PROPER VENT SYSTEM TO PREVENT CARBON MONOXIDE BUILDUP."

"POOR DRAW OBSERVED AT HOT WATER HEATER VENT. PROBABLE CAUSE IS REVERSE BENDS IN VENT PIPE. RECOMMEND INSTALL PROPER VENT SYSTEM TO PREVENT CARBON MONOXIDE BUILDUP."

"STRONGLY RECOMMEND INSTALL CARBON MONOXIDE DETECTOR(S)."

11. Furnace venting.   This item only applies to gas (or oil) burning hot water systems. Observe the condition and workmanship of all visible areas of the furnace vent. Carefully inspect the vent system for leaks, dents, improper bends, and especially too long of a run through too small of a vent pipe.   Some common comments:

"VENT HAS LONG HORIZONTAL RUN WITH MINIMAL RISE. RECOMMEND COMPLETE CHECKOUT AND TESTING BY QUALIFIED GAS APPLIANCE TECHNICIAN."

"STRONGLY RECOMMEND INSTALL CARBON MONOXIDE DETECTOR(S)."

12. <u>Fireplace condition</u>. Observe the general condition of the fireplace. Carefully operate the damper to ensure proper operation. Ensure that the size and length of the hearth is correct and that it extends far enough onto the floor (see local codes) to reduce the fire hazard. Some common comments:

"SMOKE STAINS OBSERVED ON BRICKS."

"CARPETING EXTENDS TO FIREPLACE OPENING, CREATING A FIRE HAZARD. REPAIR."

"SEVERAL LOOSE BRICKS OBSERVED. REPAIR."

13. <u>Woodstove condition/placement</u>. Observe the general condition of the woodstove (if present) and its location and placement near combustible materials (see local codes). A common comment:

"WOODSTOVE LOCATION TOO CLOSE TO COMBUSTIBLE WALL. RECOMMEND CONSULT WITH LOCAL FIRE OFFICIALS TO DETERMINE SAFE PLACEMENT."

14. <u>Chimney/flue condition</u>. With a flashlight, open the damper and look up in the chimney flue and observe any creosote accumulation or any blockage (bird nests, etc.) or and cracks in the flue. If the flue is not readily accessible from the interior, do not attempt to look down

136

the flue from the exterior (for safety reasons). Some common comments:

"FLUE NOT READILY ACCESSIBLE DUE TO WOODSTOVE VENT INSTALLATION. RECOMMEND THOROUGH CHECK AND CLEANING BY QUALIFIED CHIMNEY SWEEP BEFORE FIRING WOODSTOVE."

"FLUE NOT TOTALLY ACCESSIBLE DUE TO BENDS IN THE FLUE LINER. RECOMMEND THOROUGH CHECK AND CLEANING BY QUALIFIED CHIMNEY SWEEP BEFORE FIRING WOODSTOVE."

15. Lead Paint Test (extra). In houses built before 1978, always insert the following statement:

"PRESENCE OF LEAD PAINT UNKNOWN. IF CONCERNED, RECOMMEND COMPLETE SCREENING BY LEAD PAINT SPECIALIST."

16. Radon Test (extra). If radon is a problem in your area of the country, use the following statement on all reports:

"RECOMMEND RADON SCREENING TO DETERMINE IF RADON HAZARD IS PRESENT."

CHAPTER 7: POST-INSPECTION PROCEDURES

7.1 FINISHING THE WRITTEN REPORT

The following procedures are recommended to be used at the conclusion of the physical inspection of the property:

1) <u>Inform your client</u>. Inform your client that the inspection of the house is complete, and that you now need their address information. Using the report cover sheet, ask the client for the correct spelling of their name, their current mailing address, and phone number. Once complete, inform your client that you need to go back to your vehicle to compile the report, and that this will take approximately 10 minutes.

2) <u>Go to your vehicle to complete the report</u>. Proceed to your vehicle to finish the report and to make the report presentable. Once at the vehicle, the following items will be accomplished:

    a. Neatly fill in the rest of the cover sheet, including the approximate age of the house and date of the last significant rainfall.

    b. Quickly go through each section of the report to ensure all items have been covered. Make sure all checklists are filled in and that comments are complete.

c. Carefully count the pages. Write the number of pages on the cover page.

d. Sign the cover page. If you are a P.E. or registered architect, carefully stamp the cover sheet with your state seal. Be sure to seal so that part of your signature touches the seal. Be sure to place the date inside the seal. If you do not have a seal with your printed name, print your name beside or under your signature.

e. If you are using two-part NCR reports, separate each page copy and place the report pages in the proper order. If you are not using two-part NCR paper, get an extra cover page and fill it in just like the other cover page. Note: The Inspection Agreement MUST be two-part NCR paper. Be sure to place the yellow copy of the agreement just after the cover page (as page 2). You keep the original white copy of the agreement for your records.

f. Collate the report and place it neatly in the report cover.

g. Mark the fee and mileage on the upper right corner of your copy of the cover sheet.

h. Put some engineering paper and your pen on your clipboard. This is to help answer any possible questions by using sketches or diagrams.

i. If necessary, use a breath mint or spray.

j. Go back to your client to present the report.

7.2 PRESENTING THE WRITTEN AND VERBAL REPORT

At this point, you are now ready to present the written report to your client. This presentation of results is called the verbal report. Remember to always speak clearly, intelligently, authoritatively, confidently, and professionally when presenting the report. The following procedures are used for presenting the report:

1) <u>Find a private location</u>. If anyone else besides your client is present (current homeowners, realtors, etc.), ask your client to step aside with you. Privately ask the client if he/she would like anyone else to be present for the verbal report. Some clients want everyone present, while some clients demand privacy.

2) <u>Show the bound report</u>. With the bound report against your clipboard or on a table, say **"Here is your report."** Open the front clear cover and say **"This is the cover page. I need you to verify that your address information is correct."** After allowing a few moments for review, point to the appropriate place on the cover page and say **"Okay, I estimate the age of the house as (__) years, there are (__) pages in this report."** Don't say anything about the "Date of Last Significant Rainfall" unless there were visible problems with roof or basement leaks. Putting this date on the report helps to protect you from a personal liability standpoint, i.e., if the weather has been dry for an extended period, you would not have been expected to find leaky roofs, crawlspaces, or basements at the time of the inspection.

3) <u>Review each section</u>. Go over each section one at a time. For each

comment, state which item it applies to and read your comment word for word. Most comments should be self-explanatory, and some comments will require you to go to that section of the house to point out exactly what you found. In some cases, you can skip over certain sections because you may have already covered them with your client during the course of the inspection. Don't forget to go over the good points of the home, too, even though there may be no comments on good points. Answer any questions confidently, thoroughly, and accurately. Remember - if your client asks for contractor recommendations, state that you avoid any possible conflict of interest and that you recommend that they get three estimates and go with the contractor they feel most comfortable with.

4) Inquire about a Radon Test. While on the final section of the report, ask your client if they would like a radon screening test (only if you offer radon testing). Explain that this is a 48 hour test using two canisters, and that you need to collect these canisters in approximately 48 hours. If the client accepts, perform the next step, and then place the canisters as required.

5) Provide a summary statement. After the last section, close the report cover and provide a general statement of the home's condition. Some common general closing statements may be:

"Overall, I think this is a well-built house in a nice neighborhood."

"Overall, the main problem areas seem to be the electrical system items and storm drainage. Otherwise, it appears to be a solid, well-built house."

"Overall, it's going to need a lot of cosmetic work, but the basic systems appear to be in good shape."

"Overall, the structure is in good shape, but the electrical and plumbing systems require some fairly extensive work."

"Overall, this is a well-built house with good electrical, plumbing and mechanical systems."

Then hand the report to your client and say **"Okay, here's your report."**

7.3 COLLECTING PAYMENT

At this point, the inspection and reporting is now complete, and you are ready to collect payment. This is a simple step because you already went over the payment terms with your client when they signed the inspection agreement.

When presented with the payment check, take a quick glance at it to ensure the date, amount, and signature are correct. If not correct, politely ask your client to correct them.

Deposit the check as soon as possible to reduce the chances of it being returned. If the check does bounce, immediately call the client, explain the situation, and make arrangements for proper payment. If payment is still not received, contact the realtor or settlement attorney/agency as soon as possible in an effort to collect your payment.

7.4 CLOSING THE SALE

After payment is collected, say to the client: **"If you have any questions about the report, please call me at my office."** After the client acknowledges this, extend your hand for a handshake, shake hands firmly, smile and say: **"Okay, thank you, and the best of luck in your new house."**

The inspection is now concluded and you promptly leave the property.

CHAPTER 8: SUMMARY

The information presented in this book has shown you how to startup and operate a successful home inspection business. Hopefully, many of the tough questions that most new home inspectors have been covered. You are encouraged to follow the many useful tips and the step-by-step home inspection and reporting system outlined in this book. Many real-life lessons have been applied here.

If you do not feel comfortable using the exact procedures in any part of this book, then just change it to something that makes you comfortable.

Once you get started in the home inspection business, you should always strive to learn more and more about the technical and operational aspects of the business. You should become a "sponge" for any information or knowledge in the home inspection field. Read every book or magazine article that even remotely applies. Attend every training seminar you can afford. Remember-- you can not afford to stop learning!

Just following the procedures outlined in this book is no guarantee of success. As in any business venture, you must always stay determined, work hard, always try to learn as much as you can, and make wise decisions along the way. A little bit of luck doesn't hurt, either.

Best wishes to you--- and Good Luck in your new venture!

APPENDIX A: Suggested Reference Material

The following reference materials are recommended for inclusion in your reference library and for continuing education purposes.

BOOKS

1. CABO One And Two Family Dwelling Code by The Council of American Building Officials (CABO) (latest edition).

2. The Complete Book of Home Inspection by Norman Becker, P.E., 1993.

3. The Home Inspector's Bible by J.V. Scaduto and M. J. Scaduto, 1993.

4. Basic Engineering For Builders by Max Schwartz, 1995.

5. Diagnosing and Repairing House Structure Problems by Edgar Seaquist, P.E., 1980.

6. The Home Buyer's Inspection Guide by James Madorma, 1990.

7. The Complete House Inspection Book by Don Fredriksson, 1988.

8. Ortho's Home Repair Problem Solver by the Monsanto Company, 1995.

9. <u>Basic Remodeling Techniques</u> by Ortho Books, Chevron Chemical Company, 1983.

10. <u>Basic Plumbing Techniques</u> by Ortho Books, Chevron Chemical Company, 1982.

PERIODICALS

1. Family Handyman

2. This Old House

3. Popular Mechanics

APPENDIX B: Inspection Report and Copyright License Ordering Information

The copyrighted Pompeii Home Inspection Report is available for your company's unlimited use. For just **$69**, we will send you: 1) a set of blank reports, and 2) a license to copy them. All you need to do is add your company logo and/or letterhead, make copies, and use them for as long as you like. This can save you hundreds, and even thousands of dollars over just a few years!

Using the Pompeii Home Inspection Report is highly recommended to help minimize your legal risk and to help you perform a high quality, thorough inspection. It provides a relatively simple, logical, and methodical approach to use when inspecting a home. It also helps you, the inspector, to not miss anything during the inspection. It prompts you with a checklist type format to help ensure each item has been covered in that part of the inspection, and includes an Inspection Agreement to help keep you out of legal trouble.

Other types of home inspection reports are available from other companies, but they may be somewhat confusing, may not be as thorough, and they usually cost $7 to $15 for each report!

With the purchase of the Pompeii Home Inspection Report and copyright license, you will receive a master set of the inspection report (16 pages) and a written non-transferable license that allows you to make copies to use in your business for an unlimited time period.

You can purchase the blank Home Inspection Report and Copyright License by sending your name, shipping address, and a check or money order for **$69.00** to: [Note: These are 2001 prices.]

POMPEII ENGINEERS

Attn: Home Inspection Report

8 WOLCOTT ROAD

FREDERICKSBURG VA   22405

Make checks payable to *Pompeii Engineers*.

Shipping is included, and the reports are not returnable.

Your license and blank report will be shipped within 48 hours after receipt of your order.

We reserve the right to decline any request for a license.

You can also order with a credit card on-line. Just go to:

www.HomeInspectionBook.com/report.html

For the latest Home Inspection Report and Copyright License cost and information updates, go to www.HomeInspectionBook.com/report.html